MW01240783

Reviewed

Copyright © 2022 by Dolores Leckey

All rights reserved. This book or any portion thereof may not be reproduced or used in any manner whatsoever without the express written permission of the publisher except for the use of brief quotations in a book review.

ISBN: 979-8-218-10988-2

Library of Congress Control Number: 2022922553
Printed in the United States of America.

Interior and Cover Design by Crystal Heidel

First Edition

Reviewed

Scenes From a Long Life

Dolores Leckey

Acknowledgments

For the most part writing is a solitary activity. But, as in the production of a play, a lot happens off stage. So it is with *Reviewed*.

Three years ago, Tilden Edwards and his wife Mary urged me to begin a memoir.

They were joined by Dana Greene, an historian and biographer of women, reminding me that my doctor, John Tabacco, and my lawyer, Bill Murray, had in recent years encouraged the same. Perhaps they could see the end of the journey. All I could see were the challenges of aging—principally staying alive—while undertaking a writing commitment.

But when a kitchen accident required more help than I was used to, Cindy Jeffries, a nurse/housekeeper from an organization called Home Instead, eased my way with all the skills needed for me to live at home, in peace and productivity. She has a central role backstage.

And then there is Ellen Collins, herself a writer of stories and poetry and an artist, who undertook the task of editing, transforming a regular manuscript into the shape of a theater piece. In the course of our work together, we discovered that editing is a form of soul work.

My children, near and far, by birth and by marriage, contributed their historian skills to the project.

I am grateful to all.

Table of Contents

Reviewed

WE LIVE IN TIMES where restlessness, conflict and polarization bedevil our world and even our church. Who can witness to us, with "grace under pressure," as we seek to navigate a way forward amidst the chaos?

One such outstanding voice of authenticity is Dolores Leckey. In her insightful spiritual memoir, *Reviewed*, Dolores looks back on the "acts" of her rich life. She recounts to us the story of her journey and reveals to us her own story of being *called and gifted*.

Dolores Leckey's faith journey is grounded in her Irish American roots, and she tenderly recounts her childhood and adolescence in Queens, New York.

As her faith and her intellectual life develop, we get a sense of the direction her life will take. We see early signs of her life-long interest in poetry, theatre, spirituality, and a capacity to reach out in empathy to the distressed.

In adult life and in her marriage to Tom Leckey, her vocation unfolds as a committed disciple of Jesus. Early on, Dolores is excited by the vision of Vatican II and is part of a generation who passionately committed themselves to its implementation.

Her vocation to marriage and to ministry goes on to take shape in surprising but Spirit-led ways. Searching for ways to nurture and strengthen her inner journey, Dolores discovers early on the riches of Benedictine spirituality.

Her hunger for insight into the way "ordinary" lay people can "survive" in an often clerically dominated church rings true. Dolores's involvement with the Shalem Institute with its emphasis on contemplative prayer and her regular practice of spiritual direction clearly sustains her on the journey.

Dolores draws on such wisdom and strength as she moves from being a talented teacher, to an adult faith formator and then on to her extraordinary mission where she directs, for decades, the lay leadership initiatives of the US Catholic Bishops' Conference.

This "act" of Dolores's journey makes compelling reading! Dolores colorfully reveals, through anecdote and wry observations, the "inside story" of how the US Church sought to live out the vision of Vatican II. Enhancing lay people's right to reclaim their baptismal vocation as priests, prophets and leaders was a huge project.

Ahead of her time, decades ago Dolores was prophetically giving "voice" to Pope Francis's calls today for dialogue and encounter. Her narrative reveals her gift of allowing the Spirit to come alive in the "nitty-gritty" of personal relationships in that demanding mission.

Dolores recounts the ups and downs of how progress was made and the painful road blocks put in her and her staff's way. Certainly, her call to sensitize American lay Catholics—and even some bishops—to greater openness regarding the role of women in the Church and the importance of the ministry of lay people was not easy.

I marvel, therefore. at the myriad ways—described in this memoir—where Dolores lives out her vocation as a "peacemaker." She accepts tensions and disagreements and suffers them through to the end, without hiding the differences. This is an absolute prerequisite for someone who had to deal with Bishops of all "shapes and sizes!"

Reading the final section of her memoir, I was reminded of Psalm 92:14: *Even in old age they will still produce fruit; they will remain fresh and green.*

Dolores's ongoing "greening of the heart," her creativity, and her freshness shine through the final "act." Particularly, her wisdom about her own struggles with grief and the loss of those close to her, touches the heart.

Ever the poet, searching for God's presence, Dolores life now echoes Mary Oliver's lovely advice:

"To live in this world you must be able to do three things: to love what is mortal; to hold it against your bones knowing your own life depends on it; and, when the time comes to let it go, to let it go."

Dolores Leckey's beautifully written "story of a soul" certainly speaks not just to those of us inside the church. It is a testimony of hope for all those seeking, and not without suffering, the divine presence.

Brother Mark O'Connor FMS
Vicar for Communications,
Parramatta Diocese, Australia

Prologue

When I read through the first draft of this book, this memoir, I saw that the major metaphor throughout was the theater. I hadn't intended that consciously. I had simply written what emerged from the depths of memory. When I finished, I recognized the centrality of theater, in one form or another. What followed was a conversation with my editor, Ellen Collins, who pondered my discovery and agreed. And so, theater became the organizational principle. The story is told in "acts," rather than chapters, and within each act are scenes. The title is also a theater term, with the hope that readers will register favorable reviews.

In addition to a "review of life," this book is also about the experience of aging told from the inside. I have included three reflections on living in the moment. My research indicates that most writing about the phenomenon of living a long life has been from the viewpoint of observers, not as people immersed in the reality of old age. My intention is to contribute to a better understanding of what constitutes a life of meaning, at any age.

Act 1

Roots

My Irish roots date back to a distant cousin who lived in a town in rural Ireland and discovered that parsnips were not affected by the potato blight. Lena and her sister Mary made great cauldrons of parsnip soup and hung them along the lane between their home and the village, so their neighbors could survive another day. A lane in the town is named after her—Lena Lane. She lived into her mid-80s, while her sister Mary survived until around the age of 103.

It is in that part of County Offaly—with Tullamore at its center—that my father's family, the Coughlans, lived and, for the most part, died. Because the Irish could not own land, my father's father John and his brother Matthew worked as tenant farmers cultivating the rich soil of the midlands, bringing forth the fruit of the land and large families. The famine made it impossible to make a living by farming, so John left. Matthew remained behind, and the Coughlan family grew in number with branches all over Tullamore. Today, his descendants, my cousins, are doing well working in government, business, medicine, and education. They are all immersed in history and politics, but beyond the boundaries of the country that gave them life. It may be that deep rootedness of the Irish experience and the love of history that has the global embrace that has brought me to write this book of reflections.

John Coughlan (later changed to Conklin) settled in Queens, New York, where he was a groundskeeper on the Astor estate. His Tullamore farming was good preparation. He married Jane Shanky from Dublin, and they had nine children—Mary, Joseph (my father), Regina (my godmother), Helen, William (known as Willy), Anne (always called Anna), the twins Eugene and Walter, and Jane (called Jenny to distinguish her from her mother). Their home was a stone cottage near the entrance to the estate. My father drove me by there occasionally, to show me the small quarters where he grew up. He added a description of Christmas mornings with stockings each filled with one orange and a nickel.

My first trip to Ireland was in 1955. I didn't know my Tullamore roots then, only that we were Irish. It would be decades before I would learn about my grandfather's farm life and meet Matthew's descendants. When I took my trip, I was beginning a summer of study at Stratford-on-Avon, and I had a free weekend. I decided to go to Dublin for several days. The English woman who was overseeing the students in England was not pleased. Why would I want to go to such a place? I remember her saying, "We have to get you over that Irish Sea and it can't be by boat." She also told me I had to stay at the Shelbourne Hotel (in those days referred to as the "Protestant hotel," to distinguish it from the Gresham, the "Catholic" hotel).

My mother's heritage is not so well documented. The little bit we know was uncovered by my nephew who devoted the first year of his retirement to digging for family roots. My mother, who was baptized Frances Marie, later changed her name to Florence. She also changed her birth date from February to New Year's Day. She was born in Manhattan in "hell's kitchen," the only child of James Wilson and Mary Brady, who died in childbirth. Mary's mother raised Florence in the tenements filled with Irish immigrants. The narrative I heard was that my mother was also cared for by an Aunt Julia, her grandmother's sister. Mother's father, James Wilson, was killed in the Spanish American War.

So how did my father and mother meet? I don't know for sure. Various stories have been put forth, including one that says my father was a singing waiter at Coney Island and my mother was in a chorus line. I have no way to check the true fabric of the tale against the years of embroidery.

What I do know is that I was the last of five children. There was Florence (named after my mother) and Rose. They were followed by two boys—Joseph and John (always called Jack). Twelve years after Jack's birth I was born in Queens and raised in a house my parents built near a new Catholic parish, St. Mary Magdalene. The pastor, Father John Tinney, came from Tullamore. My parents held him in high regard, although there was never any socializing. He was simply a presence in their lives, someone my father would go to for counsel, both giving and receiving.

What is most amazing to me is that, as of this writing, I have lived longer than anyone on the family tree except Mary, the distant cousin, who lived to around 103. I cannot help but wonder why.

A Young Life

My early memory of childhood is of living with my parents and an Italian nanny in the family home in Springfield Gardens. My father, who worked as a public works inspector, made friends with a lot of Italian immigrant laborers and learned what can only be called "street Italian," just enough of the language to get him from here to there. He mentioned the need to find someone to care for his new—and unexpected—child, me. My mother was 40 when I was born and already manifesting signs of heart disease. Thus, Rosie came into our family. Her real name was Rose, but we already had a Rose, my sister, so she was known as Rosie.

Rosie was given a room and bathroom in our newly renovated basement—a recreation room styled in the nautical theme that so entranced my family. There was a bar shaped like a boat deck, and life preservers hanging on the wall. The furniture was all blue and white. Rosie had a bed down there and space for her belongings.

Her main duties were to keep watch over me as I played outside. Our land was not fenced, except for the back yard, and Rosie was charged with making sure I didn't wander off. To that end, she would bring out my little tin tea set and find me some dirt. I would happily dig and add water to what would become "dirt tea." Thank God no one was expected to taste the tea.

The other Rose, my sister, was married to John Erdman, a carpenter who worked for the Olsen Company. The story of their wedding was a popular family story. Supposedly, my father, already dressed in his tux, first went to a local baseball game. At home, all the women fretted that the wedding would get off to a late start, and there was a crisis about the flowers. Rose wanted to carry calla lilies, but Aunt Regina insisted on bouvardia, the popular wedding flower of the day. I, of course, was still in a crib, but later heard the story time and again. Rose (who worked for the telephone company) and Johnny lived in an apartment two blocks from our house. I recall her stopping by on her way to work, looking glamorous in high heels, a flowing dress, and a stylish hat. Always a hat. Sometimes she would fix my breakfast, because Rosie did not cook.

My sister Florence (called "Little Florrie" to distinguish her from our mother) also worked for the telephone company. Unlike Rose, she did not have a big wedding, but she and her husband Joe Kelly, a young sailor, eloped when she was 16. Their marriage was later approved by the church, and they had two children, a girl and a boy. I'm told that after his naval tour was over, he became a taxi driver.

For most of my childhood, my brothers, 12 and 14 years older than I, mainly ignored me. At least it seemed that way.

School Days

In 1939, I was to go to first grade at St. Mary Magdalene, the parish school. It was an eight-room brick building staffed by the Dominican Sisters of Sparkill, NY. On the first day, my mother braided my hair with two pig tails, braided so tight it hurt to bend my head. My uniform was perfect—a navy blue skirt, a white starched shirt, and a red tie. After coaxing me to take a spoonful of cod liver oil, a "must-do" for many years, she walked me to school. My school bag held a delicious lunch—a sandwich, an apple, and cookies. Life was good.

Until, that is, the second day of school.

That day, Sister Rose Eileen handed out a lined page folded into four columns and directed her class of six-year-olds to make a certain mark in the columns. The mark was actually the number 1, but she didn't identify it as such. I had learned my numbers, 1 to 10, at home, but I didn't think of the task as writing the number 1. Rather, I saw it as some kind of artistic challenge, and I tried to make zillions of 1s look like a fountain. Everyone received a gold star except me. My brothers thought I was hopeless.

Sister Rose Eileen grew more understanding, though, after my mother talked to her. I thought Sister was the most beautiful woman I had ever seen. She had two deep, glorious dimples which I coveted. I sat for hours with my yellow pencil's eraser end poked into my cheek, but no dimples ever appeared.

I was intrigued with the Dominican sisters who taught at St. Mary Magdalene School. In their white and black "uniforms" they looked like they inhabited an alternative universe. As I grew older, I volunteered for convent silver-polishing on Saturdays just so I could peek into their habitat. They always seemed to have time to talk to school girls, and it was not unusual for us girls to have a "crush" on a Sister. I certainly did. And I had a bout of jealousy when I thought "my" Sister preferred another girl to me. I stopped talking to the Sister and felt the deep loneliness that comes when one intentionally breaks a relationship because of ego-related assumptions. Finally, I got on my knees beside my bed and poured out my heart to Mary, Jesus's mother, whom we Catholics referred to as "our" mother. I used the title Our Lady of Good Counsel in my imploring. Somewhere along the way in school, I had learned about this designation of Mary. The title is associated with a painting found in a 13th century church near Rome, thought to be miraculous. It was in the care of Augustinian priests. Popes and saints found inspiration in the mother and child imagery, with Pope Pius XII composing a prayer to Our Lady of Good Counsel.

My prayer to her was for help in healing the breach I had caused in my relationship with Sister. In the midst of tears it came to me—apologize for your behavior. I did so the very next day, with Sister hugging me with words of gratitude. "I didn't know what had happened to you," she said.

This is my memory of my first "answered prayer." And in my writing room where I am now composing this memoir, a picture of Our Lady of Good Counsel hangs, a gift of a half century ago from my husband Tom who did not know the history of my childhood prayer life.

I usually went to Sunday Mass and Holy Day Masses with my parents, but one Christmas Eve stands out as one of the few times I walked to church alone. On the edge of my teen years, I set out for home after the service, also alone. As I passed an empty lot, I felt a presence. I looked into the dark space where the presence felt like music, though there was no sound. Were there angels present? Who knows? What I do know is that there was a freshness I identified as Christmas joy, and the freshness of that joy is still palpable.

As the years have piled up, and experiences have enriched my life, I have come to believe that angels are omnipresent, emanations from God appearing often and everywhere. And many other people recognize this as well.

When I was in my mid-70s and still doing my own grocery shopping, I was at a checkout counter at Giant Foods. An African-American girl was packing my purchases. She looked bored and was silent, except to ask, when all was bagged, if I needed help getting to the car. I said I did. We walked to my car in silence. I opened the trunk, and she put my groceries there. She then looked at me and asked, "How are you going to get these inside?" I answered that an angel would turn up. With unexpected energy, she nodded her head. "Oh yeah, they're everywhere, through the whole universe." She closed the trunk and her parting words were, "Have a nice day."

After my eight years at St. Mary Magdalene, my father sent

me to The Mary Louis Academy, one of the more elite Catholic girls' schools in New York City. He attributed the substance of his education (though he didn't attend school past 8th grade) to the sisters of St. Joseph of Brentwood and saw them as instruments of a good and blessed life. He wanted the best for me, and what he saw as the positive influence of nuns like the ones who had taught him.

I had graduated from St. Mary Magdalene School in midwinter, the result of having skipped half a grade around third or fourth grade. The Mary Louis Academy was a new adventure. Because it was located in Jamaica Estates, I often needed to take public transportation to get there, although on most mornings my father drove me on his way to work in Queens Borough Hall.

TMLA prided itself on having a rigorous academic curriculum. There was lots of Latin (no Greek), lots of math and some romance languages, lots of history in one form or another, including apologetics. The latter was included because you had to know some history to adequately defend the Roman Catholic Church. And then there was logic, our introduction into the world of philosophy. I consumed it all with great relish. That must have been obvious to the sisters, because for several summers they sent me to the Summer School of Catholic Action held at Fordham University in the Bronx. Jesuits from all over the world were there to instruct us how to convince others about the right and true road to salvation, namely the road to Rome.

The school had strict uniform requirements. We had summer and winter dresses, long-sleeved blue for the fall and winter and short-sleeved maroon for spring and early fall.

Our shoes were pumps with medium-size heels (the height sometimes checked at the front door to ensure compliance). There were stories of girls who had to hand in their shoes and wait in the main office until their mothers could bring the correct shoes. We wore hats, white berets that gave us a French touch.

Our days started in home room where attendance was checked. The class secretary carried the number to the office before we entered into the academic rigors ahead of us. I was class secretary that first year. One day I was late getting our "numbers" to Sister Fidelis, who expressed her displeasure to me. When I returned to the homeroom, the sister in charge could see I was upset. She took both my hands in hers and passed on some wisdom that has remained with me ever since. "Do not let these little mishaps cause your heart to race ahead; nothing is worth upsetting your peace of mind. Remember, God is with you." I cannot recall her name, but I can see her eyes looking into my inner self, offering calm and wisdom.

Since I was also interested in theater and speech, the sisters engaged my interests and sent me for private speech lessons, at their expense. For at least a year and a half I would travel once a week to Jackson Heights, where my grandparents had lived, to be coached by Madame Ballantine, a small woman who always wore a large brimmed hat. She lived in a first-floor apartment. My lessons consisted mostly in learning how to engage my diaphragm. She stood (all 4'11" of her) at one end of the apartment house hallway, and I stood at the other end. She would coach me to "project" from the diaphragm. If I did not perform to her standards, she would trek the length of the hallway and punch me in the chest, to remind me of where the diaphragm was, and then walk back to her spot. And so it went.

All of this was preparation for the city-wide Hearst Oratorical Contests, the subject of which was always late U.S. Presidents. In addition to working with Mme. Ballantine, I sought help wherever it might be. One year, when the subject of the oratorical contest was James Madison, I requested a Mass for him from the nearby Passionist Monastery. The secretary taking the information was a bit confused by the request. "The *dead* president?" she asked. I didn't see what was so odd about it, though she obviously did.

I was very successful in the oratorical world, and as I drew closer to the end of life at TMLA, I was winning various rounds in the Hearst competition. And then came the final encounter. My counter point was a boy from Fordham Prep with a name straight out of a novel—Langdon Tolland. The contest was broadcast on the radio, so the sisters at Mary Louis were able to hear it all. They heard the startling news that Langdon was declared the winner. The next day in my home room, Sister Regina Celeste announced the results, and then she turned to me, nodding, and said, "You did very well, but judges usually prefer boys in these matters."

TMLA was so much more than oratorical contests, though. For example, there is a whole bank of memories surrounding sweet sixteen celebrations. We had assigned tables for lunch in the cafeteria. On a girl's 16th birthday, a corsage of sugar cubes appeared. Made by the sisters? No one knew for sure. But years afterward, when I had daughters, I carried on that sweet custom of making corsages for them. And then, the three granddaughters, until my arthritic fingers required that I obtain assistance from our local florist. And sure enough, wrist corsages of sugar cubes appeared for Monica, Maria, and Grace.

Angels All Around Us

Father's Storehouse of Stories

During my elementary school years at St. Mary Magdalene, while World War II raged and my mother said the rosary constantly, my father was holding the emotional line. He always had a bright saying, and he also had a storehouse of stories about his early life.

The small stone cottage at the entrance to the Astor estate housed a cohort of first generation Americans who (as my Dublin cousin says) were looking for a way to make a buck. Pre-Depression and Post-Prohibition work opportunities were not terribly inviting. What I came to learn later was that the Conklin boys figured out that off-track betting was one way to financial freedom. And thus, my father (I presume) and then his twin brothers Eugene and Walter embarked on that road. The twins had a car dealership that was the front for the betting. Along the way, the sisters (Regina, Anna, and Jenny) thought they could make a little money too.

By the time the sisters got into the enterprise, the family was no longer living in the stone cottage but in a nice house in Jackson Heights. The girls had several phones installed in the house to help them conduct the business, and I am told that Grandmother Jane kept asking why one family needed so many phones.

My father would often take me on errands to places outside our Queens enclave into the larger world of Astoria. There I would see groups of men just standing around on street corners. Since my father waved to them, I asked him what they were doing. He said they were just waiting for action.

What kind of action? It could be the races, it might be spreading news about who was arrested for bookmaking or what the new odds were. The street corner was the conveyor of news. Years later, when I saw *Guys and Dolls*, I knew the script. I loved the script just as I loved my father's stories.

There were other tales about his days as a stagehand. He worked in the New York theaters as a union member. He didn't talk about that a lot, except to say that he let his union membership lapse—apparently membership could be passed on in families—when his son Joe showed no interest in it. But there was one story that sticks with me as a symbol of reconciliation.

Helen Hayes was on stage in a play that required her to pull a phone off the wall. The stagehand had to tie exactly the right knot for the phone to come out. Father was the stage hand, and for reasons that were never discussed, he tied a knot so tight that she could not pull out the phone. She was furious, and he was remorseful and embarrassed. Months later, it was Christmas. On his shelf at the theater was a box from an expensive men's store, and in the box was a shirt and tie and a note of forgiveness. It was from Helen Hayes.

Music

I began piano lessons at age 6, when our neighbor Mrs. Mead suggested it, noticing that I jumped rope in time. Everyone was puzzled by this, but my mother took her seriously and went about seeking to acquire a piano. The final decision was a baby grand piano, which required more space than was available in our living room. The situation was resolved by removing the wood-burning fireplace. One thing I learned from that baby grand is that Chopin waltzes can make you sound better than you are. That piano followed me through my life, boarded with my sister Rose when I married and moved to South Bend, Indiana, and then to various Virginia homes. It is no longer with me, but its replacement, studio size, sits here in my apartment.

As a teenager, I kept in touch with one of the nuns from elementary school—Sister Edith. She knew about my piano playing—the recitals, the venturing into "two-piano work." This differed from duets when both players were at the same instrument. My teacher Mrs. Smith had two grand pianos in her home. She would sit at one and I at the other, and we were off—usually into Chopin. Eventually she left the area to move to California where she married Raffael Jossefy, the American arranger for Chopin. Sister Edith decided that I needed to play for Frank Watson, a well-known pianist and organist in New York. And so I showed up for a conversation and an "audition" one Saturday, clutching my sheet music. He dutifully listened and suggested I take organ lessons which he would provide at Marble Collegiate Church in Manhattan. I assume this was all as a favor to Sister Edith.

I did need to find an organ, however, preferably in Queens. Fortunately, TMLA had an organ on the second floor, and I worked out a practice time for the period immediately following lunch. This worked pretty well until the day I pulled out the "echo" stop by mistake, and my humble efforts at the organ reverberated through the entire upper regions of the school. Sister Appolonia flew out of her geometry class to appear like an avenging angel in the organ loft.

"What do you think you're doing?"

I apologized. "I pulled the wrong stop."

"How do you expect me to teach geometry when you're causing such a distraction?"

I knew it was impossible, having my own struggles with theorems.

And so ended the brief experiment with the organ.

The Great Depression and War

On the afternoon of December 7, 1941, I was lying on the living room floor with the Sunday comics. My father was listening to a football game on the radio. The phone rang, and it was my brother Joe, who had enlisted in the army after high school when jobs were scarce. He was exuberant at the thought of actually fighting in a war. "Very little time," he said during the brief call. "There's a long line waiting to call home." My father hung up the phone and shook his head, mumbling for the rest of the afternoon, "Crazy kid." But before long, great numbers of young men were being drafted into the army, my other brother Jack among them.

Except for air raid practices when we had to draw the black curtains closed, life during the war did not seem too stressful for me. Even though meat was rationed, my father had friends in Astoria (Jewish triplets) who owned a butcher shop, so we managed to have meat on the table. My mother and I felt especially virtuous since the meat was blessed by a rabbi. The neighborhood world remained as it had always been, a mixture of rural and urban with a variety of ethnicities. We no longer had chickens in our backyard, but down the street a family had ducks. At Easter, Mother would buy duck eggs for our breakfast. They were large and flavorful, and a touch exotic. A few houses away from ours was a water tank in which lived some sort of large and noisy sea creature. We walked to buy groceries. There was the Italian grocery store, the German bakery, the Jewish deli, and the general store down the block where everything was sold from small buckets of beer to comic books. Sunday nights we would listen to the radio and have a supper composed of ethnic delicacies.

Saturdays were movie days, and in the theaters we watched the News of the World, followed by the feature presentation. These Saturday forays cost 25 cents. Often on Saturday nights my sister Rose and her husband, who played the guitar, would host an evening of song and party food. By then, Rose had three children, and they would devise games while the adults sang the latest hit tunes, many of which had wartime themes. Hal Aloma, who was in a trio that played in the Hotel Lexington's Hawaiian Room, and who was in a relationship with my cousin Mildred, would sometimes appear, bringing his steel guitar. He'd teach us children how to do Hawaiian dancing the right way, namely with an emphasis on hand gestures that told the story. My mother was always in attendance, though my father, who suffered from stomach ulcers, usually didn't attend. Music seemed to be the bond that held us safe while the war raged.

I had my supply of defense stamps, but I also had a little pile of cash acquired during the Thanksgiving practice of knocking on doors and begging for money. I used the money to buy doll clothes and other odds and ends of a young girl's world. This angered my mother who thought every dime should go to the war effort, but I didn't know how to make that happen.

Mid-week radio was focused on the War. Our neighbors the Olsens had a large map of Europe on the wall, and we would gather there with neighbors for dessert and news. We tried to figure out where Joe and Jack were. Joe and Jack were somewhere defending our country, and Mother was worried sick, wondering if the boys were alive or dead, or simply gone. Joe had been sent to England and served as a driver for various officers, and then was part of the second day of the Normandy invasion. There, he sustained a non-life-threatening wound which sent him back to England. Jack, however, saw well over 500 days of actual combat in the infantry, in the invasion of North Africa and Sicily. He was one of a small handful of men who survived those engagements, much of which involved hand-to-hand combat. Purple Stars, which designated combat injury, flanked our front door.

Jack's service took its toll on him. A decade later, when our father was dying of the cancer that had spread to his bones, I broke down, crying to Jack that we were helpless to do anything. He replied that death didn't bother him, saying, "I've killed men with my bare hands. You'll get over it." In truth, *he* never got over it. Now we can identify his condition as Post Traumatic Stress Disorder, but at that time, there were no such designations.

Shortly after joining the army in 1939, Joe had met Thelma, a young, beautiful Georgia woman. We learned of the marriage when her photo arrived with the announcement. She was a true Southern Baptist, something that sent shock waves through our family. Mother proudly displayed the photo, however, and we looked forward to meeting her. This didn't happen for a couple of years, until their daughter was born.

And then Thelma and Lolly (whose legal name was Dolores, after me) came to visit. We all fell in love with one another and embarked on the learning curve of a Southern Baptist entering the family of a Roman Catholic. After the war, when Joe was away on assignment in the summer, Thelma and Lolly would come to visit, and I grew up with Thelma's Southern wisdom taking root in me. We shared a room, the three of us, and at night before sleep took over there were many tales and stories told. This "sisterhood" relationship lasted until her death at the age of 77, and, I think, beyond. To this day I call upon some of her wisdom about the ups and downs of life.

When Mother died in 1950, Thelma asked me to guide her in the rituals of a Catholic funeral. I didn't know much myself, so I said, "Just do whatever I do." I repeated those words several other times in life, and as a result, all kinds of people (including a leader in the Unitarian church in America) received the Holy Eucharist. I don't think Jesus was upset.

My Mother's Death

The whole academy experience was deeply formative, and part of that formation was coping with loss.

In November of 1950, just months before my graduation, my mother died suddenly. She and Father had gone to Florida for a few weeks right after Election Day, as had been their custom. She had not been feeling well, and the family doctor had diagnosed some form of heart disease. He thought relaxation on the sand by the water would be helpful. But she began to feel worse. After about ten days in Florida, they headed home. Shortly after the plane took off, she suffered a massive heart attack. The pilot turned the plane around and headed back for Miami Beach, and life changed for everyone in our family. Father had planned to accompany the body home by train, but he couldn't endure the sudden loneliness. He decided to fly back.

I had been staying with our neighbors Mr. and Mrs. Mead (she of the piano lessons project). Father sent telegrams to them and to my brothers and sisters. That night when I came home from a school event, I saw lights on in our house and cars parked in the driveway. I thought my brother Jack had come to clean the floors, something he had promised Mother. When he met me at the door, though, I knew something was wrong. I thought it most likely that Father had suffered one of his ulcer attacks. Jack put his arms around me as I called out, "Tell me about Dad."

"It's not Dad. It's Mom."

The next day in our homeroom class, Sister Regina Celeste pointed to a note I had left on the blackboard. My Latin textbook was lost. According to a friend, Sister added, "That's not the only thing she's lost."

I was afraid to go to the funeral home. Jack rescued me by assuring me that Mother looked peaceful in death. And so, I entered with his arm around me. And indeed, she seemed to be at rest.

The day after Father returned home, my brothers and I drove with him to St. Charles Cemetery far out on Long Island to select a grave site. The most essential requirement was that it be near Fr. John Tinney's grave, he whose homeland in Ireland was the same village my grandfather called home. And it was he who had encouraged my parents to move to Springfield Gardens, since he was establishing the new parish of St. Mary Magdalene. And so, they are buried near one another.

I would not return to the cemetery for a long, long time, not until four months after the 9/11 terrorist attack. My husband and I decided then to spend a week in New York, remembering, visiting old friends, going to the theater, and visiting our parents' graves. At St. Charles, I stood at my parents' graves and Father Tinney's with bunches of flowers in my arms, dispensing bits of beauty and calling forth memories from deep, deep places. I could see Father Tinney half looking at me when I would visit him, seeking his blessing before a diocesan contest of some kind. His gravestone was starkly simple, nothing extraneous, like the man himself. At my parents' grave I inspected the additional names which I had added as a gift for the new millennium. My sister Rose, her husband John, and Jack's wife Kay had been added in 2000.

Several years after our mother's death, we learned that our father had terminal cancer and planned to sell the family home and build a new home Father and I would share with Jack and his family. The change was like a hurricane. It had seeds of safety, but there was also debris. My mother's death had led me to decide to give up plans to go away to college and stay home with Father instead. The decision was as much for me as for him. He would start a conversation about how a young girl like me needed to be around other young people. I would counter with the fact that I needed to be with him.

Joseph Conklin

Florence Wilson Conklin

Theology and Theater

What would I do about continuing my education? TMLA showed me a way forward. St. John's University had recently opened a new college, co-ed, unlike the other schools in the complex. There were rumors that the new school—University College—was designed for returning veterans so they could venture into higher education. Even though I was late in applying and had neither an interview nor an entrance exam, the Mary Louis sisters, who were friends of the dean Father José Pando, argued my case for admission. It worked.

In January of 1951, I began my studies at University College. My foray into Brooklyn for the first day of school was on a cold January day. I was afraid I'd get lost, never having been on the Brooklyn subway. I started out extra early. And when I arrived, I discovered the college was nothing like the gracious Georgian mansion where TMLA was housed. I stood in front of a plain brick, urban building, with little artistry, and a Quonset hut where we would eat and gather for special events. This, then, was the "student union."

Geography and what I considered a primitive physical plant were not my only challenges, however. After a lifetime of wearing uniforms, what kind of clothes were appropriate for this new level of schooling? All through my teen years, my mother had taken me twice a year to a dress shop in Jamaica where garments were brought out to the clients after careful discussion about what was desired. The routine for us was three "frocks" (my mother's term) for fall and winter and three for spring and summer. And then there were skirts and sweaters purchased at the local department store. I had no part in their selection. They simply appeared.

The bottom line? I had no idea what to wear or where to find the clothing. Fortunately, there were some girls from TMLA in my class, and they were more knowledgeable about fashion. I quickly learned that Brooklyn had several department stores, and Shopping 101 joined theology and American History.

Without being fully aware of it, my world was expanding in many directions. Besides the usual liberal arts curriculum, I found my way into the world of the theater. I auditioned all the time, not only for University College plays but also for plays at the all-male St. John's College. One year they produced T.S Eliot's *The Cocktail Party*, in which I had a minor role. There were also dramatic dialogues, scenes from plays that featured two people. I would find a partner and we would perform our dialogues wherever we could find or fabricate a stage.

Along with theater, the mysteries of theology beckoned. I took as many classes as I could fit into an already packed schedule. Some of them were technically in the philosophy department—cosmology, ontology. What doors could they open? My ontology professor, a short round man with a bit of a brogue, entered one day glowing over the fact that that morning he had been trimming his hedges and had pondered a new way into the depths of *being*. While I had no idea how this had happened, his radiance inspired me to try to learn more. Most importantly, it showed me that philosophy and theology could be *fun*. I sought ways to fit into my schedule a course in advanced theology, taught by the dean, Father Pando. And there I was introduced to the works of Garrigou-Lagrange and Romano Guardini. Yves Congar was waiting in the wings. This experiential contemporary theology led me to various lay movements such as the Grail and the Catholic Worker.

The Grail came to us, in the Quonset hut, through interesting presentations about the possibilities of apostolic work for women not planning to enter the convent. One girl, who lived in Springfield Gardens, actually entered into training with the Grail and was sent as a missionary to the Amazon and was never heard of again! A few of us decided to take a less extreme approach and volunteer as catechists for the Grail. Our students were mostly Spanish-speaking, and the catechetical site was across from the Brooklyn Navy Yard. I decided on a "reward system" for attention and participation, and gave out rosaries and holy cards to the students who performed well. This went on until the Spanish-speaking priest in charge of the program took me aside and told me to stop. "The boys are using these items in their floating crap games," he said kindly but firmly. You would think that with my knowledge of "the boys on the corner" in Astoria that I would realize that the "boys in the program" were familiar with street life.

The Catholic Worker was a different story. Our small group of theology/drama students was led by Father Pando to the Chrystie Street Worker House in the Bowery. Being a basically fearful person, I never would have gone on my own. Father Pando scheduled these "field trips" for Friday nights. That was when various guests held discussions, a project begun by Peter Maurin, Dorothy Day's Catholic Worker co-founder. Friday night was when Day would most likely be released from jail for participating in a demonstration of some kind. It was also the night that Cuban priests, personae-non-grata in their own country, would relate their personal stories of persecution. What remains vividly in my memory is the smoke-filled room where all these stories were shared, where plans for the future were designed, where faith was presented as concerted action.

Standing By

In the midst of all the new things I was learning, there was the emotional pain of watching my father die. I was also trying to balance what I should and could do when he was no longer there at the center of my life.

What would I do with my future? Not even finished with my first degree, I began to ponder graduate school. Should I go to Catholic University's graduate theater program? Father frowned at the suggestion. And then I read the works of Alan Paton of South Africa, and I longed to be in his land and join in the cause of freedom from apartheid. Dean Pando cheered this idea—he was concerned that "intellectually searching" young women would all end up teaching in elementary schools. Yet, when the catalogs began arriving in the mail, my father had had enough. He wanted my future to be a safe one. The idea of adventures in South Africa was filed away.

After his diagnosis of prostate cancer which had metastasized, Father had moved ahead with plans to sell the family home, build a new two-family home, and move. He and I would live in one part of the house, Jack and his family in the other.

Change happened quickly. For at least a year, as Father's

condition worsened and his pain grew, Jack and I devised a plan for his relief. I didn't think I could administer a morphine shot. When cries of pain emanated from Father's room at night, I would go down the staircase and ring Jack's outside bell. He would go upstairs and take care of our father. Jack was always available, never complained, never shirked. The morphine worked, and we would all go back to sleep.

The summer after my graduation from St. John's, Father was transferred to Jamaica hospital. I came home from my summer job at a camp to find the hospital bed gone, along with Father's belongings.

That fall, I began my first full-time job, teaching ninth grade English at Delahanty High School in Jamaica. It was a private school conducted mostly by former Christian Brothers. The students came from Catholic prep schools. Their problem was not behavior but getting the hang of how to take a test. The faculty's job was to get them through the New York State Regents exams.

And so, as my father entered the final stages of his life in the hospital, I entered a world of hundreds of papers to correct. I spent my days teaching my students how to write a coherent sentence and how to read. The volume of work, I later understood, served as an antidote to the pain of separation I felt at my father's imminent passing.

The New World of Work

There are two quotes that epitomize my attitude toward the vocation of work. The first is from George Herbert, the 17th century metaphysical poet. He wrote, "Who sweeps the room as for Thy laws/Makes that and the action fine." The second comes from Pierre Teilhard de Chardin, who wrote in *The Divine Milieu*, "God awaits us in the action of the moment . . . at the tip of my pen, my spade, my brush, my needle."

Even though I wouldn't read those exact lines until much later, it was their spirit that was in my mind as I began my first job at age 19. I had studied theology in my college classes, and bits and pieces of the Church's social teachings danced in my head. I was thinking about the responsibility that pay carries with it, and I vowed to do my best.

That first job was as a counselor for the New York Summer Playground Program. The unwritten job description was that I would do anything and everything. I had quite a few inner pastoral musings about this job, such as thinking that God must really want me to be a playground counselor because here I am and I don't even know the rules for volleyball. Plus, I was really afraid of flying objects—like balls! Most of all, I remembered feeling that I was on my way to Work, to the adult world. And scared as I was, my imaginative juices were running high.

PS 136, where the camp was held, proved to be a microcosm for all my future work experiences and roles—teacher, homemaker, television producer, writer, and church executive. On the playground, I met more than thirty energetic nine-year-olds. I also met my frustrations, boredom, and fatigue. But nevertheless, I discovered opportunities to stretch the limits of my inventiveness, my humor, and even my faith. The necessary tension of balancing work demands, social demands, family demands, and personal demands was first felt during those long, hot summer days. Somehow all these legitimate demands had to be held together. Balancing them all was awkward, but I knew I had to try. In the midst of the tugs and pulls there was a vague sense of vocation, of being called to do this particular work.

I was, even at a young age, beginning to see God's pleasure in the work of human hands, minds, and hearts and to see the importance of the smallest details of human life.

And my question now—is God in the work of writing this account of a long life?

How Things Come Together

1954 was a pivotal year for me for two reasons. The first was beginning a full-time job as an English teacher. The second was a serendipitous attendance at an opera party. Both would greatly inform my future.

As I mentioned elsewhere, my students needed a lot of coaching to prepare them for the New York State Regents exams. It was all work—no athletics, no clubs, no school-sponsored social life. Remembering my rich extra-curricular life at TMLA, I couldn't stand to see these students lead such a robotic life. So, with very little backing, I started a drama club. I did so with the understanding that I would receive no extra pay and the school would not fund the activity. Fine. I would do it myself. This proved to be no easy task, because for one thing, there was no auditorium, no stage.

I chose the play *The Man Who Came to Dinner* because I had acted in it in college and knew it well. I posted a notice for auditions, claimed a classroom to use after hours, and created a "stage" by chalking out a space on the floor. The boy playing the lead needed to grow accustomed to being in a wheelchair, so I borrowed one. At the end of every rehearsal, the floor had to be swept clean, and the desks had to be returned to their classroom arrangement. Fortunately, the classroom belonged to a supportive colleague who didn't freak out if anything was a little awry when he returned the next day.

The real challenge was finding an auditorium with a real stage for our actual performance. Fortunately, a local parochial school agreed to "lend" us their theater space for a dress rehearsal and one performance. A friend who was working as a stage hand for CBS Television had access to sets, so he and I set out in a moving van from Queens to Manhattan to create a living room set where most of the play's action took place. The friend's wife, an artist, painted some flats and included a window, and also did the make-up. We sold tickets, played to a half-filled auditorium, and when it was over, we had created a community. Drama Club was on its way.

The second pivotal event also revolved around theater. In March, I attended an "opera party" in the Bronx. One of my fellow students had recently acquired a stereo and was hosting a "listening" of Verdi's LaTraviata. I was the only woman in attendance. As we readied ourselves for Act One, a young man appeared, home from the army for the weekend. We all sat quietly and listened, until intermission, when the soldier—Tom Leckey—offered to help me cut up cheese and fruit for the refreshments. He told me he was home to see his parents off on a trip to Ireland. They were immigrants from the north of Ireland, and this would be their first visit home since leaving (at different times). Tom the elder was from Belfast and had been in the British Merchant Marine. Molly was from County Cavan and had immigrated with her three siblings, father, and stepmother, her birth mother having died at age thirty.

During the opera intermission, we didn't talk much, which Tom later reported he found relaxing, since he was very shy and had never had a girlfriend. At the conclusion of the opera, he invited everyone to his house several blocks away where an Irish farewell party was underway. So that night, not only did I meet the man I would marry, I also met his large, extended family who represented both sides of the "Irish troubles."

Reflection: Remembering Theater Days

In my late eighties, now, I feel the power of age. It's not so much that I have power because I am old, but rather that being old brings diminishments which will not be ignored. Indeed, it cannot be ignored. It is an exercise in living in the REALITY of the moment every day and every night.

I can no longer produce and direct plays for young people, but I can attend theater, usually with the company of my daughter Celia, another lover of theater. Granddaughters, too, cheerfully accompany me into the world of Shakespeare. I use my walker to access the Folger Theater, a replica of the original in Stratford-on-Avon. It's full of historical suggestions and, for me, memories.

In 1955, I spent a summer in Stratford-on-Avon studying Shakespeare in conjunction with a program at New York University. One of the high points was seeing Vivian Leigh play Lady Macbeth. She had long red hair and a beautiful green gown—and she owned the stage. And then there were play readings when we students from all over the Western world did "cold readings" of Shakespeare. I once read the role of Celia in *As You Like It*. The joy of that time lingered, so much so that I named a daughter Celia.

When I was teaching English at Delahanty High School, I taught *Julius Caesar*, a requirement I think for all sophomores. I still remember the scene in which Caesar is attacked and mortally wounded, and he says, "Cry havoc!" For the two years that I taught the play, however, I would have the students yell, "Cry treason!" I never noticed until I took my granddaughter Grace to see the play at Folger that the cry is "havoc." I went home and reread the play—after many years.

It is hard to read the plays now, because all of Shakespeare now, in my home, is in one volume, too heavy for me to carry and move. If I am to live a bit longer and want to have access to Shakespeare, I need several smaller volumes. What I could hold and move around twenty-five years ago when Tom gave me the *Complete Shakespeare* is not possible today.

Act ²

Moving to the Midwest

Tom and I were married in The Lady Chapel of St. Patrick's Cathedral in New York City on June 22, 1957. Two months later, we set out for the middle of the country. Tom had received the Father O'Hara Scholarship to study European history at the University of Notre Dame. With wedding gifts packed tightly into my small, hard-top convertible (Tom had sold his car to buy my engagement ring), we entered the city of South Bend, Indiana. When I saw the sign announcing that we were in the city, I gasped. This could *not* be a city. Tom then gave me a mini-lecture on the usual size of cities in the United States. This was a typical city. New York was the exception.

Within a week, we had connected with New York friends— Don, whom Tom knew through the Catholic prep school network, and his wife Mary Jane who had been my classmate at St. John's. They offered information and friendship. We secured a furnished apartment owned by the sheriff of South Bend, and I prepared for a teaching job in the public school system. Tom rode the bus to campus, while I drove my red and white car to school where my third-grade class awaited.

The 18 students were divided almost evenly between African-Americans and Hungarians (the Hungarian revolution had occurred a few years before). My previous and brief experience teaching in an elementary school had been in a school for intellectually gifted students the semester before my marriage, but I found new meaning in working with poor children. It became the beginning of a life-long learning adventure. One boy in particular stands out to me. Roosevelt, 12 years old, was a ward of the state and lived with a retired African-American teacher. He needed help with reading and with numbers, but he had the most beautiful tenor voice I had ever heard. The song he always chose to sing was "The Star Spangled Banner." At the farewell party for me, organized by the Hungarian mothers, he sang, and we both wept.

It was early spring when I left. I was pregnant and teachers could not teach beyond the fifth month. Ironically, I could be a substitute teacher (high school physical education, for example) but I was banned from regular classroom teaching. The vagaries of school systems!

We expected to be at Notre Dame for quite a few years, but Tom decided not to pursue an academic career. His plans for a doctorate were laid aside as he turned his eyes toward public service with the government. Our first child, Mary Kate, was born on the day he was to have received his MA. He forgot to tell the history department that he would not be at the ceremony, and when his name was called—over and over—people wondered if something dreadful had befallen him. Nothing dreadful, just something life-changing for us both.

St. Teresa — Doorway to a New World

When we left the University of Notre Dame, Tom headed to Washington, D.C. to look for a job, and I traveled to the Bronx, seeking advice from my mother-in-law about baby care. After several weeks of living apart, we took the gamble that the federal government was in our future. We found an apartment in Arlington, Virginia, near our old friends Mary Jane and Don. Before long, Tom was employed by the Office of Naval Research as a budget analyst. I was well on our way to a second child, our daughter Celia.

Nine months after her birth, we were attending the first liturgy of Easter in English, a gift of the Second Vatican Council. As we awaited the lighting of the Easter fire, I felt a deep, unfamiliar chill. It turned out that the chill was rheumatic fever. I spent three weeks in the hospital and many weeks at home in bed. The little girls went to NY to stay with their grandparents, and I lay in bed and read a mountain of books.

While I was recuperating, I decided I wanted to learn to pray, to really pray. One of the books I read was an autobiography of Teresa of Avila. She was a doorway for me into another world, into the interior space that centers all of us. A

Spanish Carmelite mystic and reformer, she taught me that the contemplative life and the active life can be held in tandem. In her writings, she shows how, finally, the mystical imperative is to look into God's world and notice what needs fixing.

And then to set about doing so.

This approach to a life of meaning offered itself to me as an opportunity when, in the mid-1960s, I sought help in bringing a speaker to my parish to discuss the state of racial inequality in Virginia. The priests approved of the idea, but the women's council—the most active and vocal agency in the parish at the time—had reservations. I felt blocked until one of the parish priests suggested I consult with the pastor of a largely African-American parish in South Arlington.

So, one autumn night in 1964, I rang the doorbell of the small house next to Our Lady Queen of Peace church, staffed by the Holy Ghost fathers, now changed to Spiritans. It was home to the lone priest, Father David Ray. Overhead was a large, bright, harvest moon, and in the doorway was Father Ray, reading aloud from a book of Langston Hughes' poetry. "My soul is like a river," he intoned as he waved me into the living room. "A reader," I thought, as I surveyed the stacks of newspapers and books around the space. He continued reciting the poem. This was not what I expected. What did this have to do with the Catholic Interracial Council?

When he stopped his reading, I described my problem to Father Ray, who suggested, and then urged, that I read the works of Evelyn Underhill. I had no idea who this woman was, but he explained that she was an Anglican laywoman, deceased, and a scholar of spirituality and Western mysticism. "You really need to read her," he said several times.

The next day, I went to the public library, and there she was in the card catalogue—248. There were several books, and I chose the smallest, *Practical Mysticism.* I devoured it, and to this day, I read it once a year. More recently, my granddaughter Monica has borrowed it! Underhill's thesis is that we need to find a way into the center of Reality and to live in Reality, a term she uses for God.

That library visit was the beginning of an immersion into mystical writings and theology, two factors that have grounded my life. It was a while before I understood what Father Ray had given me that autumn night, namely, the knowledge and conviction that one could not pursue a social justice agenda without cultivating the innermost part of one's soul. The Langston Hughes poem and the direction to investigate Evelyn Underhill were of a piece. I thought of the young men and women throughout the South who regularly boarded buses for sit-ins and civil rights demonstrations knowing they would be abused and perhaps killed. Why did they do it? They did it because they were raised in churches where the interior spiritual life was ignited. They knew the Spirit; they believed in the Spirit; they understood the power of community.

St. Teresa of Avila

Lost and Found — A Small Miracle

My brother Jack married his wife, Kay, a week after his return home from the war in 1945. They moved to the small house she had inherited from her father, and Jack went to work as a laborer for New York City. As I mentioned earlier in this book, when our father was facing terminal cancer, we all moved into a new two-family house. Jack and Kay (and by then two sons) occupied the large downstairs apartment, and Father and I lived in the smaller, upstairs one.

Somewhere around the time of our move to South Bend, Kay began to descend into the dark reaches of paranoia schizophrenia. Instead of seeking help for her, Jack left home and pursued a relationship with a nurse. We found this out later from his son, John. After we moved to the Washington, D.C. area, I received word from my sister Rose that Jack's children were in a city shelter. Their school had discovered that their mother could not care for them. They were then eight and thirteen.

My brother Joe was stationed in France, and he said (after much hand-written correspondence) that he and his wife were obviously the best choices to be the guardians of the two boys. He also said the boys needed passports and that a parent had to sign for them. Kay was in Creedmore Mental Hospital. Jack's whereabouts were unknown. Kay refused to sign the documents, and her doctors respected her decision. The only solution was to locate Jack. But how? New York City is an ideal place in which to disappear. Meanwhile, Rose took the boys out of the shelter to live with her temporarily.

How to proceed?

I was about to give birth to our third child, Thomas Joseph. Travel was not possible with a house full of babies. Tom said we needed an "agent" to conduct the search. It came to him that his mother Molly was the perfect detective, and I thought Sister Edith, my Dominican surrogate mother from the eighth grade, would also be useful.

They were an unusual team. Molly was not religious, alienated from the Church except for weddings, baptisms, and funerals. She viewed those occasions more as rites of passage than sacraments. Edith had been a Dominican a long time. She had a devotional life and a practical mind. But she was also partially cloistered and could therefore not travel the backroads of the city. The two of them consulted by phone.

Edith was sure that since there was a woman involved who was also a nurse, that Jack could be found. She suggested that Molly visit Mary Immaculate Hospital in Queens and speak with the director, a nun. Molly acted upon this. She didn't drive, but she knew the public transit system of New York better than anyone.

Having received a phone call from Sister Edith, the Sister Director of the hospital was expecting Molly. Molly related the narrative of what was at stake—either the boys get passports or they pass into the far reaches of New York's social services. The director said she thought she knew the nurse, and she surmised that this area was probably the neighborhood where either Jack or the nurse could be found. She then suggested that Molly follow her into the chapel where there was a statue of St. Jude, complete with devotional candles. St. Jude, at that time, was known as the patron of improbable causes. She and Sister knelt, one of them prayed, and Molly left to walk the nearby streets. By her account, she felt something at her back pushing her toward a particular building. She entered and encountered a manager who told her that yes, Jack Conklin did indeed live there. But no, she could not go to his room. He said Jack usually returned from his job as a hospital orderly around 5 p.m.

Molly asked to use the phone, and she called her husband and asked him to come with two chairs so they could wait for Jack in the parking lot across the way. At five o'clock, Jack walked down the street and nearly fainted (Molly's remembrance) when he saw her and her husband Tom. She conveyed the message that he was to appear at his sister Rose's house, or else a warrant for his arrest would be issued.

He complied. Passports were arranged. Jack was never seen or heard from again. The boys were educated in military schools in Europe and in the United States. At this writing, both have died.

When my fourth child, Colum, was born, we gave him the middle name of Jude, in memory of this improbable finding.

Jack in World War II

Weaving a Vocation

Father Ray offered me, and I assume others, resources needed to discern how marriage, family, work, and care for the world could be woven into a sense of vocation. These themes were part of his preaching. Not that I heard his exhortations on a regular basis. Tom and I remained, as was the custom, members of our geographic parish in North Arlington, a place with a different zip code and a different lifestyle. It would be about twenty years later that we would formally join Our Lady Queen of Peace. But every once in a while, we would be at Father Ray's church for Mass, usually during a time of demonstrations and assassinations. That church and its environs were central to the Poor People's Campaign which followed the stirring and memorable speech by Dr. Martin Luther King Jr. in August of 1963 at the Lincoln Memorial.

Many of us concerned citizens went to Our Lady Queen of Peace to meet college students who had come for another march. We, like other young families, gave food and shelter to the college marchers. A group from the University of Connecticut slept in our home, in corners, on extra couches, on the floor of our medium-size home which already housed four young children and their parents. It was crowded, but that didn't matter. I rarely think of those marchers in these last years of life except when I search my inner world for enduring memories. I can still see the faces of some of the students. Names draw a blank, but their generosity still feels alive.

During the years of caring for young children, creating a home that offered safety to them and, by extension, to others who entered our world, Tom and I tried to give space to the intellectual and spiritual development of all of us in the family. Reading was a big part of this effort. When the children were small, we read aloud at the dinner table, choosing stories that would engage them, such as the tales of Narnia. One of us would eat early while the other read. Bedtime at various times meant poetry reading. Now, when I begin to recite something from T. S. Eliot and am surprised that one of the children can finish my lines, I am met with the comment, "What do you expect? We grew up with those words!"

Involvement in community life was paramount during the years of and following the Civil Rights Movement. Tom was a planning commissioner for Arlington in addition to his full-time job. I was involved in various political activities and served on the board of the Northern Virginia Community College. It was there that I became acquainted with the newly established educational television station on the main campus of the college. It was not broadcasting yet when I met the general manager at a board meeting. After some conversation, he asked if I would like to be part of the start-up staff, responsible for gaining community support for this new venture. I was very interested, but there were a few hurdles.

*I could only work part-time due to having four children in elementary and middle school who needed supervision

*no night work

*I didn't know anything about television except how to turn it on

The manager agreed, and I worked twenty hours a week, no nights, until I became the producer of a series that was presented live one night a week. I learned on the job how to coordinate sound with visuals and how to improvise when the "talent" froze on camera.

Adrenalin is very important for this kind of work!

Alongside of this paid employment, I attended graduate school and did volunteer work for the Catholic church. I reviewed books, wrote articles, and gave lectures about the most exciting church moment in my history, in the history of the church, and perhaps the world—The Second Vatican Council.

The Council, which brought together all the bishops of the Catholic Church, was like an earthquake. What was deemed unchangeable underwent enormous changes. The liturgical language moved from Latin to the language of the people, wherever they dwelt. These changes, the gift of good Pope John XXIII, were being presented and voted upon by the gathered bishops at approximately the same time that the Civil Rights Movement in the United States was underway. Changes everywhere. Bishops I spoke with later told me that when they went to Rome, the Holy Spirit swept in, and their views of what it meant to be Catholic, to be a bishop, to understand what Christ came to teach, were completely upended.

When I read about local languages being used in sacraments and worship, I was giddy with delight. I decided to go to confession one Saturday afternoon, expecting the sacrament would be conducted in English. I didn't know that my parish would have a visiting German Franciscan helping out. The absolution I sought was spoken in German, but the exhortation (the mini-sermon to help one stay on the straight and narrow) was in halting English, but it was memorable. The priest focused on my desire to be a good parent, and he urged me to begin a relationship with my children's guardian angels. This actually fit in with my own leanings toward the wisdom embedded in angelology.

But no one saw how far and deep the changes would go. Liturgy was not the only way they impacted my life and the lives of people I knew. A spirit of freedom was growing in the ranks of ordinary people. The People of God was the language of the Council. Evident in so many ways and places was what could be called (to use theologian Ronald Rohlheiser's terminology) a holy longing. This longing was growing among the laity who for centuries had the role of being quiet and obedient to those in Holy Orders.

In my small orbit, this new way of thinking—this new desire—was concretized in the formation of a mother's prayer group. Sounds mild? This was a group of young mothers, except one who was older and more experienced in all ways, including ecclesiastically. The idea was to meet once a week, without a priest (this point was important), to try to learn to pray as a small community. After a few tries, we came up with a plan. Each week there would be one mother designated as "nursery keeper" in someone's home, while the six or seven of us "postulant pray-ers" gathered. The schedule called for a quieting down period, a reading of a scripture passage, and 15-20 minutes of quiet reflection, using whatever space was available in that particular home. Then we reconvened, shared insights from the quiet, and finally raised questions, problems, and desires that needed prayer. We had a final blessing of sorts and left to collect our toddlers. One important piece of this experiment was that we asked for prayers for our needs. This was noteworthy because Catholics traditionally kept this sort of thing secret (except in the confessional). But now, perhaps the Spirit was opening our hearts and minds to truth and to the power of community. It wasn't long before the mothers were sharing, at first hesitantly, about prayer influencing a situation such as a family member joining AA or an enduring family conflict on the road to reconciliation. The list could go on and on. We began to realize the power of prayer. Soon, others heard about this and wanted to join. How could we accommodate them?

At first, we stretched the walls of the meeting house and the nerves of the nursery watchers, and then came an idea—break into two groups with different leaders. This was hard because we had all come to trust one another with almost everything, we had become friends, and we would miss each other in this particularly graced time. But it happened. And life flourished.

This was all happening during the beginnings of the Catholic charismatic movement—a post Vatican II phenomenon, a kind of existential tie to Paul's letters to the Corinthians which some of us had experienced.

We were all searching. In my case, after my insertion into

the lives and writings of Teresa of Avila and Evelyn Underhill, the Trappist monk Thomas Merton rose to the surface, like cream in a bottle of milk. I had read *Seven Story Mountain*, his account of his own spiritual/intellectual journey, but this was like joining the Marine Corps of the Catholic Church. His search for deep silence struck an internal note in me. It was not unlike Teresa's discoveries, but framed more in the ways of the post-World War II longing.

How do you learn to meditate? What is contemplation?

I read. I thought. I asked questions.

In the early 1970s, I was asked to teach in the Pastoral Ministry department of DeSales School of Theology, one of the many theological schools associated with religious orders and located close to the Catholic University of America. DeSales was short for St. Francis DeSales who had written a book I had read and respected—*Introduction to the Devout Life*. The book's audience was the laity and had been written long before the exhortations and teachings of the Second Vatican Council.

The dean of the theologate was looking for a course in Methods of Adult Education in the spirit and teachings of the Council. I accepted the offer which seemed like a gift from God. It also offered me an excuse to leave the high-wired work of public television.

Seminaries and Meditation

Over quite a few years, my class at DeSales introduced me to the spirituality of Frances DeSales and the gentle scholarship of his followers. Members of the theologate community were eager to learn methodologies to bring the changes, teachings, and spirit of the Council to people in parishes and in schools everywhere. I found the seminarians to be eager students, open-minded and honest. We shared not only the content of the stated curriculum but the interests and questions of our spiritual pathways. Life at DeSales was an example of collaborative learning. One day a seminarian called me to share the news that a new kind of meditation group was being formed, in the wake of the late Trappist monk Thomas Merton. It was being led by an Anglican priest, would be limited to 20 people, and would be held on the grounds of the National Cathedral. It was envisioned as an ecumenical experience.

The seminarian thought this would be of interest to me, and it was. Unfortunately, it had already reached its limit of 20 participants.

I decided to try to stretch the limits, and I called the priest-organizer, Tilden Edwards, to plead my case. I think I may have argued along the lines of diversity. I, a Catholic woman, etc. He consented, and I became the 21st member of the meditation group that would become in later weeks and years the Shalem Institute for Spiritual Formation. We met every Friday at 7:30 A.M. in the Gentlemen's Library on the grounds of the National Cathedral.

A new door—of silence—had opened for me. A new mentor—Tilden Edwards—was on the threshold.

Tilden, now in his mid-80s, had studied anthropology at Stanford University in California and then, in response to a quiet inner urging to encounter God somehow, somewhere, had entered Harvard Divinity School. Ordained, he moved to Washington, D.C. and found himself at the center of urban living and urban seeking after God. The issues of social justice were always present to him as "doing God's work." He also became aware of how that work often led to burnout, even in those whose intentions were pure and honest. He came to the realization that the spirit side of the mission was not being attended to, and could feel the lack in his own being. And so began a pilgrimage into the world of contemplation and spiritual awakening. He arranged for a sabbatical from active ministry to study in California with a Buddhist monk who led him, an activist, into the quietude of deep prayer. Tilden's life turned a corner then. He returned to Washington convinced that without cultivating the inner spirit, the outward task of bring about change—conversion—would fail.

It was, in a sense, what propelled the civil rights activists in the South, the same truth that Father David Ray spoke to me about in the 1960s.

The meditators sat on the floor in the library. In session one, we spoke our names, told how we had learned of the group, and explained why we wanted to be a part of it. Then Tilden led a meditation, and speaking aloud ended. It went on like this for months, and I came to feel closely bound to my fellow meditators even though I couldn't remember their names and even though we never socialized. We met, we meditated, we left. Silence framed us as a community.

Word traveled about the group, and the following year Tilden discerned that an additional group was needed. He would continue to lead the "originals," and he asked me and the psychiatrist Gerald May to co-lead a new group. Gerald (Jerry) had joined the first group toward the end of the year, making him the 22nd member. He was working in a prison, treating people with deep troubles, and during the course of his work realized that those who were getting better were not doing so as a result of his treatment. Something else was at the center, something he later named as grace.

Before too long, the meditation groups had increased in number, and other spiritual resources were added, such as spiritual direction. A new entity was born—Shalem. The word translates as wholeness. I continued my seminary teaching and introduced a new program of studies at the suggestion of the seminary president which we called Extension Theology. The program was aimed at interested laity and was an early preparation for lay ministry, an idea so new that few people would even utter the name.

It was then, in 1977, that I received a call from a search committee at the United States Conference of Catholic Bishops, as it is now called, asking me to apply for a new position created as a result of the Second Vatican Council. A new secretariat was to be established with a focus on the laity, the non-ordained. I was told the search had been on for six months without raising a suitable candidate.

I was not looking for a job. The seminary work was fruitful and promising, with a new program on the horizon. I was happy with my work with Shalem. However, I agreed to send a resumé and to appear for an interview.

I met Tilden for lunch at the Shrine cafeteria on interview day. He cautioned me about getting into a bureaucratic position in a time of my life that he referred to as "creative." I took out a small map to pinpoint exactly where the Catholic headquarters was located and set off. I really knew very little about the organization.

1312 Massachusetts Avenue was a dimly lit building, which made me wonder if the church hierarchy was observing President Carter's request to reduce electrical use. That wasn't the exact reason, but since most of the senior staff was at the White House witnessing the signing of the new Panama Canal treaty, lights had been lowered.

Reflection: July 2019 – Patriotism

This Independence Day in 2019 opens the door to streams of memories about the importance the holiday has assumed in my life and my family's. Today, Washington, D.C. and its environs where I have lived for sixty-one years has a different feel. People are on edge. The usual celebrations of impromptu picnics and the national fireworks and concert are overshadowed by a military theme with large tanks and flyovers from the Air Force. There have been expressed fears that the occasion will be one of partisan politics instead of remembrance of the courage and fortitude of our founders who did indeed risk their lives and fortunes to declare freedom from the rule of Great Britain.

During my childhood, July fourth usually meant some home-based fireworks, except for the years when we were at our Oakdale summer home. There, somewhere on the river, the sky was ablaze with larger displays. One knew this was a different day.

Over the years, the Declaration of Independence took central stage in my growing family's life. One year, my husband Tom, an historian, took us on an excursion to Charlottesville, specifically to visit Monticello, the home of Thomas Jefferson, the writer of the Declaration. He loved to visit historic places, but I usually bowed out. This time, I was convinced that the trip would be worth the effort. And so, it was.

The interior of the house, which holds all kinds of inventions crafted by Jefferson, had a palpable "presence." This wasn't the stage for a man's life—it was an extension of his life. I began to feel that if I were not careful, I would bump into him.

The most impressive and lingering remembrance was the small burial spot in back of the mansion where Jefferson and several of his close conspirators are buried—as they had requested. Knowing they were putting their lives and their fortunes in grave danger, they decided that whatever happened, their remains would exist together.

Over the years of marriage and the creation of our family, Independence Day acquired a kind of centrality among holidays. This was perhaps because Tom's historian heart moved from the intellectual appreciation of the document to its emotional power. And the family moved with him.

Each year, there was the reading aloud of the Declaration, and each family member old enough to read had a portion of responsibility. Year after year, more people were added until eventually a large group would gather and participate in the group reading. When Tom died in 2003, two weeks before July 4th, the emptiness of life without him became even emptier as solitude wrapped itself around the holiday. I remember sitting alone at the dining table with the large dictionary open to the text ("We declare these truths") marked in his hand for various readers. I sat and read aloud—alone. Later in the day, on a trip to the cemetery, I saw at the gravesite a copy of the Declaration atop the stone. Who? One of the children? A friend? Whatever—there was still life in our ritual.

Act ^{3}

Quilt Made from Honorary Degree Hoods

Called and Gifted

I spent my first days on the job reading *Origins*, a publication of the Catholic News Service. An international synod of bishops was underway in Rome, focusing on religious education. *Origins* was publishing the "interventions" of American bishops. I had no idea that sometime in the future these interventions would matter mightily to me. The Rome synod ended, and my work began. An enriched experience of Church awaited.

Previously, my only experience of a bishop had been at my confirmation. This occurred at that time when, on the cusp of adolescence, it was deemed that one could use the movement toward maturity as the final stamp of Christian service. The exception was, of course, for ordination or taking religious vows.

Choosing a confirmation name had been a sign of this emerging maturity. I chose Catherine because I was fascinated by Catherine of Alexandria's horrible death on a wheel that tore her apart. Of course, I didn't want that to happen to me, so my back-up saint was Catherine of Siena, illiterate for much of her life, who told the pope he was not doing a good job. I later learned that I had been baptized on the feast of that Catherine, which came to mean a lot to me. My friends and I lived in fear of the "slap" which the bishop delivered during the sacramental experience. I don't remember the name of the actual bishop, but he frightened me sight unseen.

And now I was working for 300 of the same, with arch-bishops and cardinals in the mix.

As I write this, Shakespeare's birthday is on the horizon, and as I recall twenty years of working for and with bishops, I think of Will Shakespeare's observant words:

All the world's a stage,
And all the men and women merely players;
They have their exits and their entrances,
And one man in his time plays many parts,
His acts being seven ages. (As You Like It)

So many men walked across the stage of leadership in the Catholic Church in those early years post-Vatican II. It was a time of experiential learning for me, both as cast member and audience.

One of the most memorable was Albert Ottenweller, elected in 1978 to succeed Edward McCarthy of Miami as chairman of the Laity Committee. McCarthy handed over to Otten-weller the major task of writing and gaining approval for a pastoral statement on the life and work of the laity in the Catholic Church. It would be the first national statement on the laity since the Vatican Council issued its Decree on the Laity in 1965. The idea of a fifteen year "memorial" of the laity decree was very alluring. Ottenweller served on the McCarthy Laity Committee and was well aware of his desire for a pastoral statement with national backing. But first, he needed a committee of six more bishops to aid him in this endeavor, along with several lay advisors. He called me, his new staff person, to come to Steubenville (where he was the newly appointed bishop) to help in the recruiting.

Albert, as I came to know him, was reputed to be the tallest member of the U.S. hierarchy. You could envision him standing under a basketball hoop and just dropping the ball where it was supposed to be. He was like that during my work life with him, and was also a Mid-Western honest man, free of pretension.

That first meeting was filled with clues about how he wanted us to work collaboratively. We were putting a committee together. He would bring up a name, talk about the man, and seek my reaction. He'd ask if I had any other suggestions. I did not—I hardly knew any bishops. We came up with—and he hoped it was a joint agreement—a slate of six and a secondary list should some decline the invitation. Albert started phoning. *No one declined.* By the time I left Ohio late in the day, the committee of seven was in place.

Albert wanted the first meeting to be free of "the usual work of meetings." He wanted the committee members to get to know one another and to assess the level of support for the laity and their evolving role in the life of the Church.

A retreat setting in Pittsburgh was selected for an overnight retreat. By that time, I had a staff person, Paula, who was secretary, administrative assistant, and so much more. We had met months before at a retreat, and we were a perfect fit. I knew nothing about bureaucracies, and neither did she. We believed we were working for the Catholic bishops as a vocation. She was not even a Catholic at the time.

That first gathering of the new Bishops' Committee on the

Laity started with each bishop relating why he had agreed to serve on this NEW committee. Their narratives were so full of truthfulness and hope and their own life experiences in their spiritual journey that I told Paula to stop the recording. What was being shared was much too personal and heartfelt to be in a printed record.

From that moment on, the committee set out to script a pastoral statement on the laity, and one could sense the effects of the Vatican Council on their diligence and commitment. And they wanted to get the lay advisors to meet with them immediately. So, together, bishops and laity crafted the document that would come to be known as *Called and Gifted*. Privately, we called it the "miracle statement."

At that time, 1980, the Conference procedures required that a document that was to be recognized as an official teaching of the American bishops go through a specific process. First, it had to be approved by Conference leadership who drew up the agenda for the semi-annual general assembly where voting took place. In September of 1980, Albert was in Washington for that meeting, where the document would either be approved or rejected for the general Assembly vote. It was, needless to say, a stressful time for Albert and the other bishops on the Laity Committee, and for me as well. We had all devoted so much time, energy, faith, and hope in this new pastoral statement. Staff was not present for the agenda crafting and approval, but Albert relayed the first "miracle."

The president of the Conference at that time was John Quinn, archbishop of San Francisco. In the morning session of the meeting, he announced that there was a very heavy schedule needing votes in November and suggested that the laity statement be postponed to another time. The bishops were asked to vote pro or con when their names were called, but Albert raised his hand and requested a secret ballot. His request was granted. The result was, that by one vote, the laity pastoral statement was approved for presentation at the November General Assembly.

When Albert relayed this to me during the lunch break, I suggested he let me buy him a sandwich and a beer at a nearby pub favored by Conference employees.

And then November came, with amendments from bishops leery of giving away authority to the laity.

We worked on the amendments, agreeing and denying. Many of them had to do with the use of the term "ministry" to describe lay men and women undertaking tasks formerly reserved for the ordained. There could be "nothing big" like hearing confessions or witnessing marriages. However, laity were undertaking administrative and teaching roles that had formerly been reserved for the ordained. The drama was being rewritten in scenes that spoke of change.

The morning that the laity statement was to be voted up or down, Cardinal James Hickey of Washington, D.C. voiced a concern that one of his staff (the director of the Doctrine secretariat) had not been consulted about this new document. He insisted it had doctrinal implications. This staff person, a priest, was questioning the term "ministry." Albert, the cardinal, and Kelly (the general secretary who was actually facilitating this meeting of hundreds of bishops) asked me point blank if I had consulted the monsignor. I had, and I said so.

"Do you have a paper trail? Kelly asked.

"Yes," I replied. "Memos and responses, in my files at the office."

Kelly said, "I'll arrange for a long coffee break, and you will take a cab, get the file, and hurry back." The meeting was at the Capital Hilton, a short distance from the Conference office.

Cardinal Hickey read the memos and withdrew his objections. I don't know how he voted, but I learned how to use a coffee break to achieve one's end.

The document passed with the cumbersome title of *Reflections on the American Catholic Laity, 1965-1980*.

The following Saturday I was at home in a recovery of sorts when the editor of *Origins* called saying he wanted to print the text as the lead article the following week. "Summarize, please, what the document is about." I explained that it was really about the laity having a true vocation, as true as the vocation to the priesthood or religious life. I said it was premised on St. Paul's teaching that everyone has gifts to share with church and society (1 Corinthians).

Editor David Gibson offered, "You're talking about the laity being called and having gifts." Indeed. And so, the document became *Called AND Gifted: The American Catholic Laity*.

The next several years were spent spreading the word about the new pastoral statement—the small miracle. The term "ministry" was given life in the Church lexicon.

Travels With Albert

In 1981, Albert was invited to Vienna for a European conference of bishops engaged in promoting the laity. He was told he could bring a lay consultant. The U.S. Conference was willing to pay for Albert's travel but hesitated when he said he wanted me to accompany him. Finally, the Conference president, Archbishop Roach of St. Paul/Minneapolis, said he thought it strange that the one laywoman secretariat director could be held back "for a few dollars."

Albert had invited a long-time friend, Msgr. Edward Herr (hereafter known as Eddie), to come along. This lovely man was as short as Albert was tall. They were something to behold. As we were gathering at the airport, we learned that Albert had an expired passport. Lufthansa Air would not let him board. Tom suggested I call Cardinal Cooke, the Archbishop of New York. I had met him in Rome in 1980 at the Synod on the Family. But first I wanted to call the Associate General Secretary, Msgr. Daniel Hoye.

Dan laughed. "I told you so," he said. He had previously cautioned me that Albert was not known for details. Dan called the Apostolic Delegate to the United States, who phoned the airline. An agreement was struck—when we landed in Stuttgart for refueling at 6 a.m. the next day, Albert would go to the American consulate and get a temporary passport.

When we landed in Germany, I signaled to Albert (sitting several rows behind me) that it was time to get off. "Too early in the morning," he replied, and smilingly decided to let it go. Upon our arrival in Vienna, the police were waiting for him. I found an official airline person, a very efficient-looking woman in uniform, and told her we had a problem. "I know all about your problem," she replied. "It's Ottenweller!" "But where is he?" I asked. She said that he was in custody, of course, with a look of angst on her face at having to deal with such ignorance.

Eddie and I stood by helplessly, awaiting whatever resolution might happen, when we saw Albert walk out of a holding area. The Vatican had intervened, and Albert was released on the condition that he get a temporary passport in the next few days. This was essential, as Albert and Eddie had planned to travel to German to visit a psychiatrist friend.

Two snapshots stand out from the Vienna adventure. The first is of a luncheon hosted by the Vatican for all the attending bishops and their consultants. Among the throng was a bishop from Hungary, which was under Communist rule at the time. We all gathered in a sun-room with glasses of wine and a certain level of conviviality. When lunch was announced, we all had to squeeze through one door, with much pushing and pulling. I was pulled to a table along with Albert and the Hungarian bishop. There was no space there for the Hungarian consultant, who was "minding" the bishop, but a member of the Vatican Curia did find a seat. He happened to speak flawless Hungarian. And so, we were invited to ask the Hungarian bishop questions, and the Vatican could give them an informal report about life in Hungary circa 1981.

The other snapshot is of a boat ride. Albert wanted to take a trip on the Danube. The only possible time was a mid-week afternoon when there would be a major presentation by the German bishop in charge of the Laity Secretariat in Rome. We had all received copies of the lecture in our native languages the night before, but the German bishop would read it aloud. The speech was long. Albert's plan was that he and Eddie and I would sail on the river during the speech.

We set out, purchased tickets for the several-hours-long cruise, ready to enjoy the leisure. Then I couldn't find Albert. In a state of reasonable consternation, I asked Eddie to help me locate him.

"Oh, he's at that table in the corner hearing confessions," he responded. Hearing confessions?

It seems he got into a conversation with a woman who told him she was upset about her standing in the Church since she had recently married a divorced man. Word got out, and before long there was a small line of men and women seeking counsel and absolution. This was pure Albert, living out his original call to ministry. People were at the center of his life.

No one at the official meeting mentioned our absence.

Albert left the Laity Committee in the U.S., but he never left my mind and heart. When he retired as Bishop of Steubenville, his plan was to return to Toledo, Ohio where his life of service had begun. After he was settled in Toledo, he called me with details about how to keep in touch. He also related the story of his departure from Steubenville.

The diocesan bishop always has an aide, in Albert's case a religious brother who made sure phone calls were noted, the gas tank was filled, and liturgical garments were in their proper places. After the new bishop was installed, Albert was preparing to be on his way to Toledo. He looked around for the brother to fold his liturgical robes. He was not in sight. And then Albert saw him attending to the new bishop. Albert's new lack of status hit home. As he started to drive away, he was overcome with tears. Pulling off to the side of the road, he had a talk with himself. "Albert, grow up! You are on your own now, except for God who has always been with you." He related this to me with a caution—do not depend on status to determine your identity.

Albert died in his late nineties. Before his death, he continued to keep the flame of the Vatican Council alive, giving retreats in jails and conducting workshops on "From Patriarchy to Partnership," which he co-led with a nun. He was always available for encouragement and laughter.

His successor as chairman of the Bishops' Laity Committee was James Hoffman, bishop of Toledo, a canon lawyer with a different style but the same caring spirit as his predecessor.

What is there about the Midwest? this New Yorker often muses.

A Roman Holiday

1980 is vividly present to me, not only because *Called and Gifted* was approved, published, and began its journey through official Catholic life, having far-reaching consequences, but because it was also a time of personal and family challenge.

My daughter Celia, who had been studying in New York City, met and married Peter. They met at the law firm where they were working as proof-reading partners. Peter was a graduate student at Columbia University, studying Russian. He would bring his grammar book to the office, and there Celia began her foray into the Russian language—as well as her relationship with Peter. Within a short time, they were married in a little Catholic church in the Bowery next to a homeless shelter for men. Father Phil Murnion, a well-known priest with whom I had collaborated on several projects, performed the ceremony. Tom and I were able to offer hospitality to all at the wedding at a post-wedding luncheon at the Algonquin Hotel. As our son Tommy noted, "Things will never be the same." Indeed, it was a notable turning point for our family. Our oldest, Mary-Kate, was living in New York City, a student at the conservatory at Circle in the Square Theater. Tommy, the ultra-observant one, was en route to his first year of college at

Notre Dame in South Bend, Indiana. History repeating? That left Colum as our only at-home child. Tom was scheduled to undergo bypass surgery to solve cardiac problems, the result of two heart attacks in his early forties.

And then . . . the international synod of bishops, earlier announced by John Paul II (now a saint), was about to take place in Rome in October. The topic was marriage and family, and it was at the top of the Conference's agenda. A delegation was being formed of bishops and periti (theological experts). And while my official role was as director of the laity secretariat, it was deemed appropriate that I, as a woman, should be one of the periti. I presume the thinking was that since women in marriage and parenting were all laity, someone in the delegation should fit that role. The three other periti included two priests and a lay theologian who was the father of five.

When the question was raised to me, I hesitated. How could I leave my husband in his surgical recovery period? Once again, my mother-in-law Molly stepped in. Before I left for Rome, Tom would be at home, and she would arrive to take over the household. The surgery was scheduled for early September, and departure for Rome in early October. Tom was sure this would work; I was not so certain. We brought the dilemma to a Missionhurst priest who had been guiding us in recent years as a spiritual director. Father Arthur agreed with Tom that it was all possible. The Spirit would provide.

The delegates, elected by the body of bishops, were Archbishop John Quinn of San Francisco (president of the Conference), Bishop Francis Stafford (chairman of the bishops'

Family Life Committee), Bishop Sanchez (representing the Latino community), Archbishop Joseph Bernardin (later to become Cardinal Archbishop of Chicago), Father Donald Conroy (director of Family Life), David Thomas (a lay theologian specializing in marriage and family), and a Jesuit moral theologian from Chicago. The latter was especially important to Quinn who was moving toward an intervention regarding birth control.

There were several preparatory meetings of delegates and periti. One held at the University of Notre Dame was to identify the major issues the American bishops wanted to address, and would do so. By the conclusion of the meeting each bishop had settled on the subject he wanted to work on. Quinn wanted to focus on birth control, while Bernardin was interested in the psychology and spirituality of the cycles of intimacy. Quinn also wanted an intervention on the changing role of women in general. He asked me to prepare a paper on the topic, which I did happily.

Kelly had arranged for me to stay with the delegation of bishops and other periti at Villa Stritch on the edge of Rome. It was a residence of small apartments (bedroom, sitting room/study, bath) for American priests and visiting bishops. It was obviously all male, except for the nuns who were in charge of housekeeping and cooking. Once again, I would be the only woman in an all-male setting, a situation not unusual for me. But this time I felt uneasy, even anxious. Maybe Tom's health situation contributed to the unease, or maybe unfamiliarity with *complete* clerical culture was overwhelming. I asked Kelly if I could stay in a nearby convent and come to the villa each day, just as I would to my office. Kelly paused, and then said slowly and deliberately, "Do you know what I went through to get you in there? Don't leave me hanging."

Shortly thereafter, I traveled to Rome with David Thomas. Kelly was already at the villa and greeted us graciously, and then, scanning my travel outfit, suggested I might want to "dress" for dinner. This, the first night, was important, he said. "After that, you can be casual."

It was arranged that I would sit opposite Quinn, president of the Conference. It was a place of honor at the table and would signal to one and all that I was on equal footing. That evening I met the residents, priests of different ranks who worked in various curial offices. Most of them would go to the bishopric, a few to the Cardinalate, and a sprinkling would return to their dioceses for pastoral work—their original calling. I understood that my presence, not just for one dinner. but for a month of dinners and breakfasts, presented some challenges.

On that first night, to say that John Quinn was a quiet dinner companion is an understatement. Like many of the priests, he would be rightly identified as an introvert. Whether this was by personality structure or the need to be cautious in speech was hard to tell. As the evening went on, one priest named Edward Egan (later Cardinal Archbishop of New York) took an interest in my work with the synod now underway and noted that I mused aloud that I needed to refresh my Latin. This was casual dinner conversation on my part, but the next morning I opened my apartment door to find a Latin grammar with the regards of Msgr. Egan. This was important learning for me—that the rich diversity of human life expresses solidarity in different gestures as well as in different languages. As Egan moved up the hierarchical ladder, his introverted personality did not win him friends, but then they were not the recipients of his attentiveness to personal need. I was, and I was grateful.

As the bishops prepared their interventions into the Synod proceedings, three of us (David, Fr. Don Conroy, and myself) were busy arranging strategy meetings with the Canadian periti. The fourth American peritus, a Jesuit moral theologian, considerably older than the rest of us, did not attach himself to this triumverate—wisely. The idea was that the Americans and Canadians could comprise a sizeable voting block when the time came. But to do so, we needed to construct a joint strategy. This was not easy since the Canadians were carrying on their work in two languages, English and French.

I had not yet discovered the writings of novelist Shirley Hazzard, an Australian who was a close friend of the English novelist Graham Greene. She and her husband usually spent time every year with Greene on Capri. She even wrote about it in a memoir titled *On Capri with Graham Greene*. The book is an invitation into the private lives of writers and artists who found Capri nourishing to their life and work. I had, however, encountered Tom Burns, editor of the London Tablet in the 1980s who was instrumental in Greene becoming a Catholic.

Before I left Washington for Rome, Burns had contacted me about having lunch sometime during the month of the Synod. I happily agreed, not pausing to wonder why he would want to. We met at the Columbus Hotel where the English liked to stay in Rome, on the road that led directly to the Vatican.

After soup and pleasantries, which included the story of his long-time friendship with Greene, Burns raised the possibility of having lunch with the American delegation at Villa Stritch. To what end, I wondered. He said he wanted to give them the stories and analyses published by *The Tablet* at the time of *Humanae Vitae*. It was known that John Quinn would be speaking on that subject, and Burns said he simply wanted to provide some helpful material. I said I would explore the possibility.

I took the request to John Quinn who was very open to the idea. He said I should check with the sisters about the details. And then the rector of the Villa heard about it and summoned me to a meeting.

"What do you think you are doing?" he asked, not too kindly.

"It's just a social occasion with a respected international journalist," I replied, adding, "I checked with the Conference president . . ."

He came back with, "If he writes one word about the Villa, you're fired!"

I passed that on to Tom Burns, eliciting assurances that silence about life in the Villa would be observed to the fullest.

The bishops' mail cubicles were filled with useful information from *The Tablet*: a variety of statements and analyses from bishops and theologians world-wide, including Pope Paul VI's recognition that more reflection and dialogue would happen. The Americans were not lacking information, and, as far as I could tell, were enjoying the company of the English journalist, godfather to Graham Greene, even if his Winston Churchill accent made him hard to understand.

Next on the agenda was the final preparation of Quinn's presentation to the Synod. He came to the Synod having served earlier as chairman of the Family Life Commission. He had listened to priests describe the problems and dilemmas with which good and faithful Catholics were struggling every day. He was acutely aware that in 1980 a major pastoral problem facing the church was how to help lay faithful and the priests who ministered to them understand the full teachings of *Humanae Vitae*. Because he trusted the expressed word of Paul VI and John Paul II, his intent was to respond in an adult way to the invitations and requests extended by these successors of Peter. Twelve years after the issuance of *Humanae Vitae*, he posed a question that desperately needed honest study. Were the only options available to the teaching church silence, repetition of magisterial teaching, or dissent?

Quinn didn't think so. There was an aura of hope about him as we met prior to the Synod session on the topic. He had several suggestions for dealing with the impasse. He asked that a new context be created, one that emphasized church teaching on the responsible transmission of life and that articulated in a positive, biblical way the church's comprehensive teaching on sexuality. He also suggested that the Vatican initiate a widespread dialogue with Catholic theologians throughout the world on problems raised by dissent from the teachings in *Humanae Vitae*. And he asked that careful consideration be given to the process by which magisterial documents are written and communicated.

The night before Quinn made his presentation to the Synod, all of us listened as he read the paper aloud, slowly, sentence by sentence. After each sentence, he asked for agreement, disagreement, or discussion, whatever was needed for all to be able to support the statement. When he went to the aula the next day, he went with unanimous support of the American delegation. Everyone understood it to be a responsible statement of fact with intelligent suggestions for dealing with a very real and growing pastoral problem.

We were shocked the next day, as was the whole Villa Stritch household, to read the AP morning headline: *Quinn Challenges the Pope*. The story that followed had never happened. Both Quinn and Bishop Kelly issued clarifications, which somewhat set the record straight. But Quinn was not available for press interviews or panels. It took a week or so before he was willing and able to face the press, but when he did, he made his position clear. He understood the Church to be a living organism, the body of Christ. To be alive is to change. He emphasized that the Church is not a museum. The delegation and staff were proud of him for his straightforward presentation, and for the underlying impetus that powered him to take this stand for the peace and stability of the people and their priests.

Before the official closing of the Synod, he submitted a written intervention on the changing roles of women in church and society. It did not garner much attention then, but it later became a foundational piece of future teaching about the role of women, at least in the American Catholic Church. The conclusion of the Synod and Quinn's time as president of the Conference coincided, and I rarely saw him afterward except in passing. The last time I saw him was in the early 80's in San Francisco. I was there to deliver a paper for the international ecumenical group, Laity Exchange. He heard I was in the neighborhood and invited me to lunch at his residence. I knew how hard it must have been for him—he was a genuine introvert—and I knew that in honor of Christian community and a bit of shared history that I should accept. Quinn himself answered the door, and then he, a layman on his staff, and I sat at a table for a quiet and somewhat strained meal. But even while I was eager for it to be over, I recognized the difficulty he must have had in extending this gesture of hospitality.

Another example of Quinn's reaching beyond his normal barriers concerns his relationship with Bishop Kenneth Untner of Saginaw, Michigan. Untner served on the Laity Committee. He was bright, inspired by his mentor Cardinal Deardon of Detroit and breaking long-held clerical customs. I was surprised to read that Quinn preached at Untner's funeral. How could that be? They were so different in their theology and in their styles. Or maybe not as different as I thought?

I learned that Untner once went on a sabbatical at a California retreat center staffed by Sulpicians. Quinn was living at the center in an apartment, as the retired Archbishop of San Francisco. When Quinn heard about the sabbatical, he extended Untner an invitation to live with him in his apartment, larger quarters than Untner would otherwise have had. In his final illness, Untner requested that Quinn, who had become his friend, preach at his funeral. Who would not want a friend—a true friend—to say some last words about you?

Synodal Side Trips

In between working sessions at the Synod, I managed to slip in a few excursions. The first was a trip to Capri.

The weekend before John Quinn was to give his intervention on birth control—i.e, Paul VI's *Encyclical Humanae Vitae*—we three Americans and three Canadians set out to visit the Isle of Capri. How did we decide? We asked our Villa Stritch hosts where they would go if they had two free days. Capri won. We went off late Friday afternoon in a rented van to a port of sorts—Venetre du Mare. Window on the sea. Our plan was to stay overnight there and the next day take a boat to Capri. Our group confused the innkeeper. Five men and one woman. Who went with whom? He assigned the bridal suite to the French Canadian priest and me—but that obviously wasn't going to work. Finally, after English, French, and Italian explanations, I took over the suite—alone and missing Tom.

The boat ride to Capri was uneventful, but that changed after the landing. Don, David, and I went one way, the Canadians another. Capri—sea and sand and rocks—was breathtaking. However, we made a serious mistake by standing too close to the breaking waves which crashed over all three of us. Father Don was thrown upon the shore sans shirt. I was pulled under, and the wave claimed my earrings, my sunglasses, and nearly my life. I couldn't get up from the waves. Then David, who had not been thrown down, reached for my hand while steadying himself on a rock sharp as a knife. His hand was cut badly, but he saved me. We were frightened and confused, and each somewhat bloodied, but from behind a large beach rock a German couple appeared with a first aid kit and tended to our various wounds. They advised us to climb the long stairway to the upper level and find a hostel and a good restaurant

The Canadians' day was normal.

The second excursion was a trip to Castle Gondolfo. One Sunday afternoon, Bishop Stafford, Archbishop Sanchez, Father Don, David, and I "borrowed" one of the hired Mercedes on hand for the bishops' daily trips from Villa Stritch to the Vatican meeting hall. We were headed to Castle Gondolfo, the summer residence of the pope. We thought we might be able to get a little tour. As we pulled close to the residence, the bishop spotted a runner jogging down the street and ran up to him for an unexpected renewal. It turns out they had met in their seminary years. The jogger was George Coyne, the Jesuit astronomer, who oversaw the Vatican observatory. He invited us all in to the castle—the pope was away—and we toured the observatory, had drinks as the sun set, and then set off for dinner in a family-run restaurant. It felt a little bit like a "the cat's away so the mice had a great time at play" experience. We felt invigorated for the final Synod days.

On another day, one of my last days in Rome at the Synod's end, a member of the Curia who lived at Villa Stritch asked me if I would like to have a "shopping visit" before departing for the States. He said he would drive me to a piazza he knew well, in his remarkable antique car. Just to be polite, I agreed. As we walked around different shops looking for scarves, he talked to me about a painting of Mary Magdalene who had visited Caesar shortly after the crucifixion of Jesus. Her purpose, according to legend, was to inform Caesar about the horrors visited upon a good and holy man, Jesus of Nazareth. It was customary to bring Caesar a gift at the time of audience with him, and Mary Magdalene brought a red-painted egg. She explained to Caesar that she was poor and could not afford anything "grander," but the egg told the story of blood shed for no purpose. She also explained that Pilate was responsible. Of course, I wanted to see the painting, but my escort said that the painting was not in Rome, but in Jerusalem. It would be many years later that I would see it on a sabbatical in Jerusalem.

But the most special Sunday, for me, was spent in a small village outside Rome. Msgr. Jan Schotte, CICM, who was then an official with the Pontifical Council for Justice and Peace, and who years before had been a chaplain for a Christian Family Movement group to which Tom and I had belonged, invited me to tour the hillside towns outside Rome. David Thomas joined us. In one village we saw a procession with the entire town either in the procession or cheering from the sidelines—all save one man. This middle-aged man sat far out of harm's way reading a newspaper. "He's the Communist mayor," said Msgr. Schotte laughingly.

The town itself was situated dangerously at the edge of a cliff, and simply living there must have been an enormous act of faith. We drove further up the hillside (or was it a mountain?) until we came to a village so still it seemed to be wrapped in silence. No one was in the streets. It was as if the population, whatever its number, had experienced the rapture. And then, suddenly, there was a sound, something falling against the stone alleys, echoing like musical notes. Nuts.

Nuts were falling from the trees in gardens and on walkways. The silence magnified their sound. A door opened and an old woman stood for a moment on the threshold, and then with a smile beckoned the monsignor inside, and by extension, David and me. I felt very hesitant, but Jan took my arm as we moved inside a small house filled with barrels of nuts. We all sat at a long table, the woman offering us wine and nuts, smiling all the while. She was hospitality incarnate. She and her brother made their living harvesting nuts, and she was sharing her substance, her life, with us. The village lives in my memory as a place of holy silence and nourishment. Lines from a Jessica Powers poem fix the image for me.

Here you are, pilgrim, with no ties of earth
Walk out alone and make the never-told
Your healing distance and your anchor hold
And let the ravens feed you.
                              –from *Counsel for Silence*

Voices Heard

Everyone thought there would be another synod in Rome in the mid-80s, and that the subject would be the life and mission of the laity in the Church. The topic fell squarely into the Secretariat I had been hired to lead. Bishop Stanley Ott, chairman of the Laity Committee, thought we should undertake an extensive consultation with the laity, to get the benefit of personal experiences, hopes, and problems. Ordinary people leading ordinary lives. How to reach them, especially those who were not active in organizations and movements?

The answer was right in front of us—diocesan newspapers all over the country. We decided that I would write an article that asked this question—where do you experience Christ in your daily life? Most, and perhaps all, of the papers printed the article and asked readers to write to the Laity Secretariat about their experiences. We had no idea who was in the readership, or if there would be any response.

And then—more than we had hoped for. People wrote long letters, some even filling notebooks. One reader said, "I have been waiting for someone to ask me."

Analysis revealed that the primary "place" where people experienced the presence of Christ was in their families. And all kinds of families, not just the high-functioning models. One woman wrote that after years of being in a brutal and hostile marital relationship, she found the courage to leave, realizing there would be people who would listen to and support her.

The next most frequently mentioned place was the parish, and especially the sermon. The Catholic News Room was amazed, since so many complaints about preaching were often heard. But many of the responders mentioned being away from the Church for months or years and then wandering into an 8 a.m. Sunday liturgy. And something happened. The hardened newsroom people, who had heard everything, were astonished. I heard one say, "That poor chap probably put his early morning sermon together between the rectory and the church." Maybe so. But something had touched the writer, and maybe others. The workings of the Spirit are not confined to a particular method.

Another surprise response was the workplace. People wrote of their spiritual experiences in places where they labored. This was of interest to me because there was a stream of lay leadership in the post Vatican II Church which objected to the growing emphasis on lay "ministry." They identified this with the loss of the true lay vocation, i.e. to be a saving influence in the paths of society.

The challenge before me and my colleagues was to see and appreciate the two emphases—ministry in the church and work in the world—and to see and understand them as being in tandem. We decided on a second Catholic news article, this time focused on work. "Where, if at all, do you encounter God in your work?" I asked. And the responses poured in from all walks of life. I began to understand the power of narrative theology.

A man who fixed home furnaces wrote that when he descended into the half-darkness of basements, he had the opportunity to see and appreciate the intricacies of spider webs. In the quiet of the basement, without pressures to hurry, he encountered the amazing work of creation, and it drew him toward that which we name God.

Another, a house painter, wrote of making a space beautiful and realizing that he was, in a small way, participating in the ongoing creative work of God. The same writer spoke of doing some touch-up painting and not charging for it—a gift to the Creator.

This kind of inquiry is not over. In our current digital age (some call it the digital axial) searchers after the Divine are called to explore new frontiers beyond those in which many of us were raised. This is the challenge of a living church, rather than a museum.

Second Time Around

My second tour of duty as a perita was to the 1987 Synod on the role and mission of the laity. It was so different from my synodal "baptism" in 1980. First were the living arrangements. The male periti stayed at the North American College where promising seminary students were sent. I was assigned other quarters in a building next door. It was occupied on the first floor by a group of Mexican nuns and on the top floor by an American nun who served as librarian for the College. The upper quarters consisted of a common room with a magnificent view of the grand avenue leading to the Vatican, several bedrooms and baths, a kitchen, and a balcony. It was perfect. Sister Librarian was away most of the time I was there, but she let it be known that guests would be welcome. And so, my husband Tom came for ten days, other visitors from America and elsewhere dropped in, and social gatherings of one kind or another were usual. It was Rome at its best. But there was also work.

The General Secretary, Msgr. Daniel Hoye, who had a few years earlier worked in one of the small offices in my original lineup, was now managing the whole enterprise. Refreshingly so. He was a cleric not interested in hierarchical ladders but in helping the staff do their work as well as possible. We traveled to Rome together. He had been given two first class tickets (so he thought) when actually it was one, which he insisted I use, and which I insisted he use.

On our first night in Rome, we went out to dinner, and I fell asleep. I think my head was slipping toward the marinated mushrooms, which I still remember, all these years later, as delicious. After two weeks, Dan decided he had had enough, that it was time for him to return to the U.S., and I as senior staff was in charge. This was a lot more than checking on theological correctness.

There were many social events that the American bishops hosted, which I was to oversee. Mostly this meant that French or Canadian delegations came for lunch. Everything was very polite. But one event involved the Brazilians who, like the Americans, represented a large conference of bishops. Cardinal Bernardin was more of less in charge of this, although he was not President of the U.S. Conference. He asked me to oversee the luncheon arrangements. This included finding a Portuguese translator/interpreter because most of the Brazilians did not speak English, and our delegation neither spoke nor understood Portuguese. One idea occurred to me. Various orders had missionary offices in Rome, and one of them must certainly have language skills. I knew the OMIs (Oblates of Mary Immaculate) were headquartered not too far from our College, and so I made an appointment with the President of the Oblate College.

I explained my linguistic needs to him. "Perhaps," I said, "you could point me in the right direction?"

"Well, I speak Portuguese," he replied, "but you should

know that I don't like nor do I want to be involved in church politics."

In all sincerity I answered, "That won't happen, I assure you. This is a social occasion only. We've welcomed other delegations, and it's all been pleasant and friendly."

With that reassurance, absolutely sincere on my part, the OMI president agreed to come for lunch—and translation.

And so, lunch was served, and not a political phrase was uttered until the first sip of coffee when Cardinal Bernardin of the U.S. and Cardinal Lorscheider of Brazil said, in different ways, "It's time to discuss the appointment of bishops."

Bernardin requested that I ask the OMI translator to stand so everyone could hear well. He stood, and he looked at me as if I were a traitor. He left as quickly as he could after being reminded that the conversation was considered confidential.

I don't want to suggest, however, that the 1987 Synod was mostly about lunches, dinners, and cocktail parties.

There was the hard work of dealing with two difficult issues in the contemporary church—the reality of a growing lay ministry (with the need to express the underlying post Vatican II developing theology) and the historical and growing important recognition of the laity's vocation to life in the world. The position articulated by the American delegation was that these two engagements of lay life were not incompatible. Indeed, both had commitments to ecclesial ministry and work, life, and relationships in the social sphere. One of the questions that we, in the Conference of Bishops, pondered all the time was the validity of both forms of service in the church.

Closely related was a second issue—the role of women in both expressions of ministry. The American bishops had launched a study of this question in the form a pastoral, *Letter on Women in the Church*. In addition to the standing Committee on Women, a writing committee was formed and hearings were held around the country. The bishops who attended these hearings and learned about the experience of women in the church and society were deeply affected. And the listening bishops conveyed what they had heard to their colleagues who were delegates to the Synod. These two issues—defining ministry and women's place—formed the undercurrent of the Synod.

Ordination was bound to be a topic, and indeed it was. An eastern rite bishop from India offered the experience of his own ordination to bishop when he was given the authority to ordain women to the diaconate, adding that he had never done so. Fast forward to 2020 and note that Pope Francis has established a commission on women in the diaconate. Thirty-three years is not a long time for significant concerns, like ordination, to receive the Church's official study. There is a long-standing acceptance of slow walking and the belief that it will eventually get you to the finish line. In 1987, the main American presenter on the subject of women was Archbishop Rembert Weakland, supported vocally and spiritually by Cardinal Basil Hume of Great Britain. Like Cardinal Hume, Rembert was a famous Benedictine monk. Furthermore, he was a superb pianist and had been Abbot Primate of all monastics world-wide prior to his appointment as Archbishop of Milwaukee. (It was a shock, therefore, when he admitted in the post-Synod years to a homosexual relationship with an actor years before. He had used diocesan money to pay the man in question not to publicize the fall from grace.)

After his retirement, which was formalized in a penitential service (as befits a liturgist), Rembert wrote a memoir, *A Monk's Tale.* I reviewed it for a Jesuit publication, and in my introduction revealed my long-standing friendship with him and added that it was probably a good thing that he fell in love—a humanizing experience for anyone like him with a formidable intellect. The cover-up got out of hand. What should be noted, however, is that Rembert's memoir is a truthful tale. It is not the whole truth because no one, including the principals, knows the complete truth. But there are no lies in his account of his life, his ministry, and his fall. In this year of 2020, one can forget how life-giving the truth can be. No hyperbole, nor blaming, nor contrived reasoning. No lies. Light in the darkness.

Meeting New Challenges

Perhaps because all women are canonically "lay," the decision was made to expand the secretariat which I headed. In a swipe of a pen, the Secretariat for the Laity became the Secretariat for Marriage and Family, Laity, Women and Youth, and Young Adult Ministry. This meant that upon my return from Rome I had to find and secure staff for these added responsibilities—everything not associated with ordination. Marriage and Family was surely a priority somewhat shaped by the Synod of 1980.

The director of Marriage and Family for the Archdiocese of Baltimore was interested. Together with the bishop (the chairman of the committee on that subject), myself as director, and someone from the Office of the General Secretary, Rick McCord was interviewed. He was easily the universal first choice, and despite his home in another city, he was ready to undertake all that this new position required.

He not only dealt with the multitude of issues regarding family life, he proved to be a wise and intellectually equipped colleague to discern the next steps in a plethora of issues. One, of course, was how to address the ordination of women.

The pastoral letter, *Women in the Church*, a project that took years of study and writing, went down in defeat in

1992. Bishop Joseph Imesch, who had led the effort for approval, knew ahead of time that there were not enough votes to pass this latest (of many) drafts of the pastoral. The negative votes were coming from the more progressive wing of the Conference which objected to the closure of all discussion about ordination. When Imesch presented his document, representing nine years of work, he said, "Because we, bishops, cannot adequately respond to the issues and concerns raised by Catholic women across this land does not mean the issues are going away." The pastoral was a closed subject, but the question of women's roles was not. Two years later, on the feast of Joan of Arc, Pope John Paul II issued a document on women that appeared to eliminate the possibility of ordaining women. The Bishops' Committee on Women, now part of my (and Rick's) responsibility, was meeting in California. My suggestion was to issue a press release that said we would still be working toward recognizing women's essential role in the Church. It was June, and the general meeting would not happen until November. What ensued was an honest and spirited discussion about this latest (and apparently final) obstacle to enlarging women's role. During a break, I said to Rick that we had support for a press release. He replied, "Why not go for a full statement in November?"

"Why?" I pressed.

"Because these bishops—our committee—had a spirited discussion on the topic. Isn't one of our roles helping our bishops tackle difficult issues?" He suggested starting a larger conversation with more bishops than just those on our committee.

This meant we needed a document ready for September, if we hoped for a vote at the November General Assembly. It fell to me to author it.

Drawing on St. Paul's letter to the Ephesians, I read and prayed for direction, something that could serve as a discussion starter for the ordination question without banishing the statement in its infancy. The key seemed to be in the fourth chapter when Paul brings to a crescendo the Christ reality of the many gifts given to the early church, gifts that display the richness of diversity in oneness. We are members of one another, Paul wrote. We are called to peace.

That became the foundation of the statement *Strengthening the Bonds of Peace* which stated unequivocally that women and men were equal in the life of Christ. The document was approved, but not without some heated discussion and charges of feminism taking over the church. The accelerated work of producing the statement and the public endorsement of innate equality were voted for affirmatively by the entire body of bishops, with only ten negative votes. I was not surprised. What I learned from this particular experience was that small steps matter, and that I personally have a high tolerance for waiting for the bread of life to rise. This learning sustains me to this day as I try to navigate the waters of aging with wrong turns that often feel like nothing is being accomplished.

Papal Visit and World Youth Day

The "stage of life" during those years between 1987 and 1994 held so many interesting, dedicated people and so many life changes. A central player was the pope, John Paul II, now recognized as a canonical saint. He had an interest in the United States, and prior to the Synod embarked on a pastoral visit to the U.S. Each stop had a specific theme, such as ecumenism in the South. In San Francisco, the spotlight was on the laity. This was exactly the right introduction to the Synod on the horizon. The allotted time for us to talk with the Pontiff about the laity in our country was very limited. There was no time or interest in scholarly papers. How to convey the diversity, energy, dedication, strength, and holiness of the American laity in fifteen minutes?

I spoke with a filmmaker I had met prior to my work with the bishops, Martin Doblemeir, who had followed a dream of blending religion and faith with the real lives of people. He had done so successfully for many years, and in 1987 he came up with an idea suggested by the success of a recently published coffee table book—*A Day in the Life of Americans*. Martin suggested a film shoot of several stories of Catholics in America in 1987. Moreover, he wanted to do this in real time all over the vastness of America.

And thus, it happened. On a Wednesday in March in 1987 (the feast of the Annunciation, quite special to me), because Martin said it's a "working day" for Americans, for laity, five film crews filmed their subjects. It was March 25, 1987, exactly thirty years after Tom and I had met. These are coincidences I notice.

There was little time, but lots of energy, as the filming began. The subjects included a cross-section of people and places. There was a Mexican crossing the Rio Grande, holding his clothes above his head. This led to a story of the hospice that welcomed him. There was the divorced mother of several children who worked in a post office at night and described her leaning on faith and family. There was the wealthy financier with a Wall Street office who related his inner call to care for the poor and how his job helped him to do so. There was the story of a parish in the Midwest, with all kinds of people and problems, and how laity, as lay ministers, helped address those problems. It was a flag flying for the importance of a vibrant parish life.

Did the Pope learn from it? Did he like it? I don't know, but I think parishes and laity around the country felt validation for the paths of their lives of meaning.

After the papal visit and the Synod, the world seemed to rotate more quickly and with more complexity. First there was the upcoming World Youth Day to be held in Poland with the Pope present. Because of the extension of my Secretariat, the issues and problems of youth and young adults were now at my doorstep. World Youth Day required the participation of our Secretariat, so I, along with the person we hired to steer the way of youth and young adults, went as officials to Poland. I asked the "powers" at the Bishops' Conference to pay for the Laity Chair, Bishop Bob Morneau. My husband Tom and our son (with the same name) attended as paying participants. I managed to get us quarters in an old, communist-style school not far from where the various programs would be held. This was all in the small town of Czestochowa.

The trip to Poland was like a lesson of life in the bloc. We—Tom, son Tommy, and I—realized what everyday life was like there. Basically, it was hard. We made our way to Czestochowa via train, to the school that would be our home. At some point, before the events of World Youth Day began, Bishop Robert Morneau arrived looking like a pilgrim from the Middle Ages.

This was one of the first visits of Pope John Paul II to his homeland, and it was filled with awe and gratitude. I think everyone felt the power of the moment. I didn't realize that it was also the occasion of planting seeds for a World Youth Day event in the U.S. That became evident at a small dinner Tom arranged for the American delegation (which included two bishops) and a monsignor from the Vatican. We had a lovely time deliberating over six versions of cabbage, as meat was scarce in Poland at that time. At the end of dinner, Tom and I left, while my staff person for Youth and Young Adult Ministry, Paul Henderson, remained with the Vatican representative who presented a proposal for a similar gathering in two years in America. In practical terms, this meant I was to convince the U.S. Conference of Bishops to act on this papal desire. Before those discussions could take place, Tom, Tommy, and I headed for Taizé in France.

World Youth Day was over for the moment.

Small Steps and
Open Doors

We were part of a group of couples who met monthly for a number of years to study various works of Christian commitment and, often, Catholic action. I emphasize that it was *study*. It was also prayer and faith-sharing. We were all active members of the local community in addition to raising families and engaging in the cultural life of the Washington area. We existed in communion to strengthen our outreach. And then came the call from the penitentiary in Richmond, Virginia.

One Sunday morning on our way to Mass with a newly-formed Eucharistic Community (NOVA), we received a call from the Catholic prison chaplain about a man whom all the chaplains believed would be a good candidate for parole but who had no family or anyone on the outside to put together a parole plan for him. Could we—Tom and I—help?

We took this request to the Community Mass and said we would travel to Richmond to meet the man. If it seemed the right thing to do, we asked if we could expect support from the community. We knew we couldn't do this alone.

Several people signed up to help, and Tom and I went to

Richmond to meet Jerry. He had lived almost entirely in some sort of institution. First an orphanage, then juvenile jail, and finally the state penitentiary. As Tom and I entered the outer lobby, awaiting the arrival of a chaplain or two, we saw a display of instruments of restraint on display. I froze and became fearful. I didn't want to go further. The chaplain kindly talked me into a less anxious state, and Tom assured me all would be well. Then we entered a world unknown on many counts. The calls and whistles of the incarcerated didn't help.

Our final destination was the room where the men being considered for parole met with the board who would recommend or deny parole. For the first fifteen minutes, the Chief of Parole, Tom, and I were the only occupants. I sat in a chair that was nailed to the floor. Nervousness filled the air of the room. We were informed what while Jerry looked kind and harmless, he had purchased a gun prior to a planned robberly, had fired the gun into the James River to make sure it worked, and then proceeded to initiate the crime.

When Jerry entered the room, he took my nailed-down chair. I don't remember the particulars of the conversation, only the sense that here was a man with a good heart. We liked him and agreed to work on a parole plan.

When we returned to Northern Virginia, a small group of NOVA members formed a support community, and together we worked on finding a place for Jerry to live and a job to help him make his way on the outside. Tom and I made visits to the Good News Mission, which worked with ex-convicts and which advised us what to do and not to do. We also began a relationship with Herman, Jerry's designated parole officer in Arlington. Herman was born and raised in Austria and was a relaxed and experienced guide on the hills and valleys of helping someone like Jerry, a man who knew so little about responsible living. Jerry had earned "bad time" on his record because of his several attempts to escape. Herman's take on these attempted escapes was that Jerry showed that his IQ was higher than we thought. It was his opinion that it was smart to try to get out of jail, though he said it should be done through legal pathways.

After a while, Jerry became involved with a woman named Juliet who planned to steal antique furniture stored in empty residences. The police were called, he and Juliet were arrested, and Jerry was sent back to jail—briefly. Some kind of higher court ruling erased all bad time from his record, and he was released from the road gang. He headed back to Arlington.

I tried to talk him into taking adult ed courses, but he didn't like them. "Nobody speaks English," he would complain. Tom took a different route, choosing just to be Jerry's friend. The two of them would have coffee on Saturday mornings near Jerry's rooming house, and Tom would talk with him, and help him unravel the mysteries of life on the outside. He gave his advice about filling out income tax forms, and became a kind of coach teaching him to read.

In those days, libraries had telephone books of most cities and their surrounding areas. One day, Jerry went to the library, looked up his name in the directory for the city he remembered from his childhood. He found his sister's name and called her. A few days later she flew to Washington, D.C. and they had a reunion in his long-ago childhood place.

Jerry kept in touch over the years, letting us know he was

okay. He had a job in a state park, married, and had two daughters. He always wanted to talk with Tom (understandably) and stressed the gratitude he had for all Tom did to help him. After Tom died, contact with Jerry was lost. My memory of him, however, is not.

When I reflect on this one extended episode in my life, several things emerge. First is that a small step (in this case agreeing to go to the Richmond penitentiary) can lead to many open doors. I see how vital community support is to bolster good deeds. Without the other couples' support, we would have collapsed in mid-stream. I also personally became aware of how fear—in my case the fear of entering the jail—could cause one to reject a pathway to God's love. This is a lesson that needs to be learned over and over. Paul teaches us that perfect love casts out fear, but it takes a lot of practice.

cMonastic Inspiration

Monastic life, with its silence and rituals and what I perceived as balance, was always drawing me closer, inviting exploration of a dialogue between the vocation of marriage and the Rule of Benedict, one of the most influential documents in all of history. As I studied the ordinary structures of our growing family life, a small community of six, I detected similarities with what I knew about life in an abbey, living according to a monastic rule.

I was helped by my relationship with Arleen Hynes, mother of ten, who with her husband Emerson and the children had moved from Minnesota to Arlington where Emerson served as administrative assistant to Senator Eugene McCarthy. Both McCarthy and Emerson had close ties to St. John's Abbey and College in Minnesota. The Hynes family, influenced by Benedictine dedication to vitalizing Church liturgy and consciously connecting worship with the lay vocation to energize the pursuit of justice in society, brought these values and goals to their life in northern Virginia, and beyond to the nation's capital. In the 1960s, with race relations and civil rights at the center of politics and theology, the call to Catholic Action led to both study and engagement. There were marches, house dialogues, and the weaving together of church reform and the reform of civil society. The Hynes family, with Arleen present in the community while Emerson was at work on Capitol Hill, was teaching the Benedictine way of life by example. Arleen valued learning, as they managed a household of ten (8 boys and 2 girls). They prayed the psalms daily, promoted the arts and artistic urges in family members, and read good literature. Arleen led a group dedicated to producing a workbook based on the official teachings of Vatican II. They all attended the Spiritan church where I had first been introduced to the work of Evelyn Underhill. Arleen and I both served on the diocesan Liturgy Commission, so we often took long car rides to Richmond for meetings of one kind or another. It was on those rides that she would illuminate for me how the dynamics of family life were not unlike those of life in the monastery.

That pattern took form in my first book, *The Ordinary Way*, which illuminated the connections between family life and the way of life in monasteries. Intimacy (as in friendship), stability, prayer, study, hospitality, and labor—these were some of the connectors. Over the years, others were brought to my attention, such as recreation and environmental activities. Decades after the publication of *The Ordinary Way* I met a nun who told me that as she was preparing to take her place as a novice in her order, the novice mistress gave her my book. Her first reaction was, "What on earth for? I'm about to give my life to Christ, and she gives me a book on family life!" But then she realized that both pathways were about domestic life, and as such, had much in common.

A footnote on Arleen. She was widowed in her late 50s and in her mid-60s became a Benedictine nun in Minnesota, where her married life had begun. As a credentialed poetry therapist, she did her work (labor) in that field and lived to celebrate her 25th jubilee as a Benedictine nun.

Memorable Abbots

Aidan Shea, OSB

I had known the value of a spiritual director from the early years of marriage. That role was usually filled by a priest, either diocesan or member of an order. These directors were often transferred out of the Washington, D.C. area. My friend Ruth knew I was in need of spiritual guidance, and she promised to be on the lookout. One day in 1979, two years after I began working at the Catholic Conference of Bishops, Ruth called to say she had found my director.

"He's a Benedictine monk and uses literature to illustrate his teaching. It's a perfect match. He's at St. Anselm Monastery in Washington. He led the retreat I just attended."

"Does he have a name?"

"Of course. It's Father Aidan."

I phoned, not knowing his last name, but we connected. I told him my felt need and asked if we could meet once to see if we would mesh. He agreed, and on Holy Saturday of 1979 we had our first meeting, the first of almost forty years.

In the beginning, we met once a week. After a number of years, it stretched to once a month until the last years when Aidan was dealing with the challenges of Parkinson's Disease.

Then his state of health (or mine) determined the calendar. Along the way, Aidan was elected abbot of the monastery, and I was busy with the Bishops Conference and, later, with the Woodstock Theological Center.

Of Abbot Aidan, I will say this—I cannot imagine what my life would have been like without the gift of his friendship and his gift of his ability to read the true state of the human soul. His body now lies buried in the monastery cemetery, and his spiritual wisdom lives in the communion of saints. His influence is ever-present to me and I imagine to the many he counseled over the years.

Abbot Robert Barnes, OCSO

Way out in the Virginia countryside—Berryville, to be exact—is a Trappist monastery. I discovered the monastery as I looked for what I called a "Quiet Day" in the early years of child rearing. I would drive out to Berryville, spend some time in the chapel, and visit the gift shop which had books and products from Trappist monasteries around the country. I knew a few of the monks, and everyone for miles around was familiar with the monastic bakery and especially its holiday fruitcake. For some reason, my youngest child, a son, expressed an interest in the monastery and upon occasion would accompany me on my Quiet Day outing.

Once day I received a call from Brother Benedict, the Prior of the monastery, asking if I could donate some money for a new guest/retreat house. Tom and I agreed that we could. Then another call came from the Trappists asking us to participate in a major fundraising effort. We agreed, and we soon learned that raising funds for a place dedicated to silence and seclusion is not an easy sell. It's not the same as raising money for a hospital or a school.

Soon after, the abbot, Robert Barnes, visited our home on his way to a meeting with our diocesan bishop. He encouraged our efforts, and my husband observed how hard it must be for him to show up at afternoon teas and cocktail parties, seeking donations, when normally he would be at one of the many prayer services at the abbey.

Eventually, the specific fundraising efforts reached a rest point, but Abbot Robert remained a friend and an informal spiritual advisor. I learned that in his preparation for priesthood, he studied clinical psychology which helped him with monastic leadership and also benefited ordinary lay people—like me. I recently found a letter I wrote him after a personal retreat at the abbey.

May 3, 2014—Feast of Philip and James (my Tom's middle names)

Dear Robert,

The few days spent in the quiet of the monastery, along with our conversations, comprised a wonderful birthday for me. My angel joins me in thanking the Berryville Community, and you in particular, for providing such sacred space for renewal.

I managed to get the Erikson book, the revised version, where he starts with old age—how about that? His point being exactly what you talked about, namely the integration of all the other stages and experiences as really the goal of life. This seems to me like worthwhile reflection as one gets even closer to the final event.

Easter was beautiful. The OLQP vigil began at 8:30 with our pastor Tim Hickey presiding in both English and Spanish, which was a total surprise to most of our parish community present. There is always another priest, the Franciscan Joe Nangle, to handle the Spanish. So, we learned something new about Tim. Oh yes, our other Spiritan priest, Tom Tunney (age 80), had fallen and was in the ICU recovering from emergency brain surgery. With only one baptism and a couple of confirmations, we were out by 11 p.m. My son Tom sang one of the psalms, and on the final verse sang so softly you could hear a pin drop. You can imagine my motherly emotion at that time. The next morning we had 11 a.m. brunch at Tom's house before he, his wife Margaret, and graduating senior Monica left to visit Guillford College in North Carolina. Monica applied there, sight unseen, and they offered a full tuition scholarship. It's an old Quaker college, small and personal, which is what she was looking for. It is, however, farther away than the Virginia school under consideration. I have not yet heard the final decision. Monica's younger sister, Grace, who is 15, stayed with me while the others traveled south. Grace goes to school in my neighborhood, so Grandmother's place was convenient. She spent her time here immersed in geometry and playing the piano. Except for the geometry, I thought it was great to be 15.

Here is the book of Celtic prayers I told you about. It's a good companion to the ancient rock from Iona. May it bring you joy.

Love and gratitude for everything,

Dolores

I continued to visit the monastery, in my new aloneness,

and would always have a session of discernment with Robert. Then, one day after his first trip to Europe for an international meeting of abbots from all over the world, Robert came home with a cough he thought was bronchitis.

It was cancer.

Abbot Thomas Keating, Trappist

Another monk, Trappist Abbot Thomas Keating of St. Joseph's Monastery in Massaachusetts, also stands out as a spiritual beacon. He is best known for making Centering Prayer (a form of meditation) available to ordinary men and women. His fellow monk, Basil Pennington, was his partner in this endeavor. I first encountered Abbot Thomas at St. Anselm's Abbey (Aidan's home) where he gave a presentation on meditative prayer. I kept up with his work through Tilden who invited me to visit the annual meeting of the Ecumenical Institute of Spirituality, a simple organization of Catholic and Protestant leaders who first met at the Second Vatican Council in the early 1960s.

I met Abbot Keating in person when I invited him to speak at a conference I had organized for the bishops on the relationship between spirituality and social justice. In his Trappist garb, he looked like someone from central casting. And when he spoke, his words were about encountering God beyond the images that most civilizations had constructed about the divine, the holy one. His words rang out. "You must smash every image you've ever had of God, who is NOT the image." When he finished, he walked away in silence. There was no applause. It would have been superfluous. People filed silently out of the meeting room.

Members of the press were present, and one, a woman reporter for the Miami Herald, approached me and asked if we had arranged for people to meet with the abbot privately. She said she had removed herself from church life some years ago, but she had taken this assignment for reasons she didn't quite understand. "No," I said, "we did not plan for confessions or private meetings." And then my assistant suggested we clean out the broom closet and "fix it up somehow." She went to the nun who was the director of the center and secured a wooden cross, two chairs, and some artificial flowers. They took the place of the brooms and buckets. After consulting with the abbot, we posted a notice that he was available for private meetings, including confession.

I later learned that the reporter who initiated the change in the program left the Miami Herald for work with the archdiocese of Miami. So unexpected are the leadings of the Spirit.

After the Council, over a period of four years, the theologians and observers began to explore the common ground of Christian spirituality, and they determined to find a way to continue their relationship which had so enriched their lives and work. Thus was born the Ecumenical Institute of Spirituality. It was first led by Dr. Douglas Steere, a renowned Quaker who taught ethics at Haverford College, and Fr. Godfrey Dikeman, a Benedictine monk and world-famous liturgist from St. John's Abbey in Minnesota. The idea was for a group of Catholics and Protestants to meet for four consecutive days a year in alternating religious space in different parts of the country. Initially, participants were men who had been at the Council, but soon others serious about exploring the reality of the spiritual journey were invited. One of these was Tilden Edwards.

The next logical step was to invite women into the exploration. Among the first women were the Carmelite nun Constance Fitzgerald and Dorothy Devers, a leader in the Church of the Savior in Washington, D.C., a church noted for its creative work in the area of social justice and its respect for Catholic spirituality. The pastor of that church was a gifted Baptist minister whose World War II experience as a chaplain in combat zones shaped his commitment to ecumenical living and worship. Dr. Doris Donnelly, a Catholic lay theologian teaching at Fordham University and known for her work in the area of forgiveness, was also an early member.

At some point in the early 80s, I was asked to present a paper to the group on women's revolving role in the life of the Church. Morton Kelsey, a Jungian psychologist and an Episcopal priest teaching at the University of Notre Dame, suggested he join me in the presentation. And so it was. What followed was an invitation from Douglas Steere for me to become a permanent member of the Institute. Over the years, the annual meeting was a source of genuine encounter.

Brother Roger — A Different Kind of Abbot

Taizé was a community of modern monks from several ecumenical backgrounds, committed to unity and to ministry to young people. Their founder, Brother Roger, was known for his aid to Jewish refugees attempting to escape Nazi persecution. He would personally escort them across the Alps into the safety of Switzerland. Now, Taizé specialized in programs called "Pilgrimages of Trust" for young adults. I was headed to visit him in France to convince him to conduct a pilgrimage in the United States.

On our way to the small village outside Lyon, I knew I had to convince Brother Roger to do the proposed pilgrimage not in a big American city, but in a smaller venue. My preference was a college campus, and I knew that the University of Dayton would welcome such an event. I was a member of the Board, and I knew the terrain as well as the order that oversaw the university. Also, it was in the middle of the country, which would be symbolically and practically doable. My maternal instincts wanted some kind of "control" over the thousands of prospective pilgrims.

Meeting Brother Roger on his little patch of the world, which Pope John XXIII had referred to as "that little springtime," was different in so many ways. Thousands of young people were camping out, standing on line for food, going to the makeshift chapel made beautiful through the brothers' ingenuity. Roger was like an icon in his peaceful presence. Because Tom and I were a married couple, and I was a representative of the Catholic bishops, we were given a private room which was the epitome of simplicity. On our second day we were to have lunch with Roger in a grove of trees. Our son Tom was to be included, though he had joined the regular soup line. The brothers (among the most observant people I have ever encountered) located him and we all lunched with a group of brothers in what resembled a scene from a French novel.

Aided by a perfect translator, we agreed that the proposed pilgrimage would be held at the University of Dayton. According to the Taizé method, it would take a year of preparation.

So for the next year, while I was taking phone calls from the Vatican about the proposed World Youth Day in the U.S., two of the brothers had moved to Dayton to get to know the community at large and the campus in particular. The brothers asked if they could attend the Bishops' General Assembly so they could get the pulse of that august body.

They arrived at the Hilton Hotel in downtown Washington, not wearing their usual blue jeans but their rarely donned white habits. They stood out in the staff section where they attracted many questions and not a little wonderment.

When the time came for the Pilgrimage, the brothers had assembled in larger numbers. The sports arena was converted to an inner garden, and bishops had been lined up to participate in the night prayer around the cross, a special Taizé call to conversion. The usual construct was for counselors and/or priests to hear confessions and give counseling to Protestants.

The archbishop of Cincinnati, who was uncertain about this event occurring in his diocese, later told me that the Prayer Around the Cross, with the ensuing confessions and counseling, renewed for him his original desire for priesthood. His vocation had led him deep into administration, where the original call was often too dim to hear. He had been uncertain about this novel event in his geographic home, but the experience changed him.

Some years later, during a prayer vigil in Taizé, a deranged woman came up to Roger asking for a blessing and plunged a knife into his neck. He died.

His work has not died, however. His love of the poor, his desire for unity, and his simplicity and courage continue to inspire.

Jerusalem Sabbatical

Pope John Paul II did make it to the United States, to Denver, where close to a million young people gathered. Tom and I traveled to the Mile High City to help in whatever way was needed. My particular responsibility was the Vigil Night where Maestro Gilbert Levine would conduct a youth orchestra. But the night of the concert, my heart and mind were in St. Joseph's Hospital where Tom was recovering from a heart attack, his third in eighteen years. The altitude in Denver was thought to be a contributing factor.

Recognizing that the travel which was a part of my work would be a growing concern in light of Tom's cardiac challenges, I began to think of retirement. That was not my only goal, however. I also entertained the desire to visit Jerusalem. For some time, I had been working through the Ignatian Spiritual Exercises with the help of a Jesuit on staff—Drew Christiansen. We would meet once a week and make our way through the assigned topics to which we added poetry that shed light and understanding. I had a growing desire to be in the places and spaces where Jesus had walked. At some point, I began to feel a pull toward Jerusalem.

In a conversation with my friend Dana Greene, I shared this desire. She suggested that I ask for a sabbatical, not an easy thing to do since the Conference didn't have a sabbatical policy. But with Dana's encouragement, I sent a memo to the General Secretary, making a case for a study in Jerusalem. I had in mind Tantur, an interfaith study center on the outskirts of Jerusalem and two miles from Bethlehem. My proposal was that I would have three months at Tantur, with no salary from the Conference, but that they would finance my travel and tuition and keep up my life insurance. Tom, already retired, would pay his own way all around.

To my surprise, the General Secretary agreed immediately. And so, in January of 1994, Tom and I flew from New York to Tel Aviv. During the cab ride to Tantur, we saw hillsides ablaze with lights that our driver described as protests. We soon learned that there was usually a demonstration or protest somewhere in the vicinity at all times. As we waited to be admitted to Tantur, we stood under a sky of blazing stars. I felt the truth of all those Christian hymns I had learned as a child. Would the angels soon appear? Or were they already present?

Looking back on the three months that followed, I realize that the time there was one of the happiest periods of my life, if not *the* happiest.

Why? Perhaps for the first time in my life I was free of everyday responsibility for life's activities such as studying, caring for home and children, and meeting work schedules. Even though Tom had continuing heart problems, the urgency about that seemed to fade. We were aware that Hadassah Hospital was one of the best in the world. All we needed to do was appear for classes, field trips, communal prayer, and meals that I did not have to prepare. It was an experience of relaxed and experiential learning which remains with one over time, even everlasting.

The sabbatical class was ecumenical and international, with friendships forged on the basis of our common pilgrimage. The Tantur rector, Paulist Father Tom Stransky, loved the land called holy and invited us all to likewise fall in love. On one of our first evenings, he took our group to the roof. There was still daylight, and he asked us to look in a particular direction and to "see" Ruth and Naomi coming over the hills to start a new life. I can still feel the thrill of that emerging imagination.

Stransky was the principal author of *Nostra Aetate*, the Vatican Council's major document on restoring relations with the Jewish faith. He was deeply involved in Jerusalem's ministerial association, which included Christians from all walks of life. It was natural, therefore, that he was a leader in pulling together the first Christian-Jewish conference ever held in the state of Israel. The planners had been working toward that end for years, and now the time had come. He asked me to be a presenter, first apologizing for "intruding" on my sabbatical and rest. I was assigned to lead a workshop on Christian Family in a Secular Society, and at the last minute was asked to speak at a general session on feminism.

It is generally believed that the unexpected always occurs in a land called "holy." And so it was for me. The workshop on Family Life was standing room only, including African bishops from the Anglican Communion, women from a faraway kibbutz, and a contingent from the Armenian Orthodox Church. The latter included a woman in advanced studies at Hebrew University and an American man from Brooklyn working toward priestly ordination in the Armenian rite.

After my presentation came questions and attempted answers. The African bishops were not so much interested in family life as they were in Cardinal Joseph Bernardin, who had chaired the most recent Bishops' Family Life Committee and who had been accused of sexual abuse. The young man later retracted his accusation as he was dying, and he received the final rites from the cardinal. The Africans were actually interested in a public stance against homosexuality. I'm not sure that they knew that Cardinal Bernardin had asked the Family Life Committee to write a pastoral statement to parents of homosexual children, the origin of Always Our Children. I had no further contacts with the Africans.

The Armenians were a different story. Two weeks after the conference I received a phone call from the soon-to-be deacon asking for my help in arranging a meeting with the young woman from Hebrew University. Why? Because he had to become formally engaged (or something akin to that) before his ordination to the diaconate. Otherwise, he would not be able to marry afterward.

I asked how long they had known each other. "We met at your workshop," he replied.

I was speechless. I said, "You don't know her, and she doesn't know you."

"Yes," he countered. "But this could work if we had time together."

My response was simple and direct—I'm not getting involved.

I had already been contacted by the young woman about

giving a lecture to the Armenian monastic community on the role of the laity as taught by the Second Vatican Council. The lecture would be in the presence of his Beatitude Torkom Manoogian and would be open to the public. This was like delivering a lecture to the Pope! I had agreed to that and to dinner with her family beforehand, Tom included. Note: the lecture was written in longhand in a small notebook and is included in my archives at the University of Notre Dame.

The evening was an amazing example of the learning that can arise from different cultures and historical circumstances, including the role of women in various Christian churches. I quickly ascertained that the young woman "arranger" had been looking for a way to bring up the topic of women in the Armenian church, and this occasion offered a step in that direction. I never mentioned the phone call from the deacon-in-waiting. Years later, when I was no longer at the Conference, she contacted me. She was married and living in New England. We were never able to arrange a meeting, but her initiative lingers in my memory.

A quarter of a century later, I wonder about the role of women in the Armenian church, and I remember having a childhood playmate, Evelyn, who was Armenian. We would play at "saying" Mass at her house. A small table was the altar, we were both priests, and her mother gave us pillow cases to cover our hair. We used Ritz crackers for communion bread. We were very reverent and serious, and it was lots of fun. When Evelyn moved away, there was no more play-acting.

My final role in the conference consisted mostly of quoting Pope John Paul II who frequently said, "Papa est feminista," which caused ripples of laughter. I also recall Tom introducing me to feminism through Simone de Beauvoir, a French woman writer. As a student in Catholic schools for most of my academic life, feminism had not turned up as a "positive." This led to many interesting conversations, some of them quite heated and laced with old theology on my part. The audience seemed to understand the conundrum.

For both Tom and me, the sabbatical was a time of true sabbath. We were together in a land of mystery and faith, free to read and learn, and to meet others seeking a deeper infusion of what gave meaning to our lives, without the daily responsibilities of work and home. I don't think we ever felt so alive. New acquaintances from different cultures became fast friends, and there was a freedom to try new and different ways of thinking, believing, relating. We put up notices:

Shall we go see the Chagall windows at the Hadassah Hospital chapel?

Anyone want to attend the free rehearsal of the Jerusalem orchestra?

How about on the first Sunday of Lent we walk from St. Catherine's monastery in the desert to Jericho with Sunday Mass on the rocks along the way? Surely one of the priests in our group will have a Mass kit!

And so it was.

When Holy Week was over—Easter so memorable—Tom and I left Jerusalem for home. It was the only time I cried leaving a far-off place. Tom assured me we would return. It never happened, except in memory.

Via Dolorosa

Affordable Housing

During the 1980s, we had been part of a group of four couples who met to pray, share faith, and discuss our responsibilities to the community in which we lived. As part of our gathering, we decided to study the U.S. Bishops' Pastoral Letter, *Economic Justice for All*. We began to ask questions about the meaning of that document for our community of Arlington County, Virginia. What we saw was the lack of affordable housing for people with jobs—beginning teachers, emergency room nurses, firefighters, even our own adult children! We asked to meet with the County Manager to see what we could do help with this situation. He said that while there were several non-profit organizations focused on housing, the need was so great that another non-profit would be helpful.

Each couple put $250 on the table, and with $1000 the Arlington Partnership for Affordable Housing was born. Thereafter, we begged and borrowed resources to enable us to purchase old garden apartments coming on the market, rehab them, and preserve them as affordable rentals. We couldn't afford office space. The Leckey dining room served that purpose, and Tom acted as the Executive Director, unpaid but determined to get the project off the ground. We put together a Board of Directors and discovered how vital the word "partnership" was in our title. The County donated staff support, churches gave us tithes, and we discovered religious foundations that helped non-profits get mortgages at very low interest rates. We invited commercial builders to be part of the project, and they accepted. A partnership was a reality. Within a few years, we were able to have a "real" office and hire a director from outside the founding group.

After our Jerusalem sabbatical, Tom donated his time and experience to support the new director, and bit by bit we were able to purchase properties before new high-rise builders could take over low-rise apartments. With support from the state of Virginia, other non-profit groups, a variety of churches, and a citizenry that believed Arlington should be a better place for everyone, APAH continued to grow in many directions. At this writing, the organization is growing outward into neighboring Northern Virginia counties and is recognized as among the best run non-profits in the United States. Much of the credit goes to the exceptional directors who have cultivated the small seeds of beginning into a flourishing enterprise.

Tom in His Painter Overalls

Reflection: Crisis

2020

The world today is one filled with worry and attempts at understanding and conquering the mysterious ways of the Covid 19 virus. It's summer—high summer—as I write this. There is a national discussion underway about whether schools at all levels can or should open for the fall semester. Almost everyone is scared. The national response borders on chaos, and one wonders if decisions, minimal though they may be, are being driven largely by political desires. A presidential election is the big item on the fall calendar.

I've been attending virtual Sunday Mass for almost five months. I like it despite the lack of direct human contact. Slowly, more people can attend in the church building—the maximum at this writing is thirty. One calls for a "reservation" and is then assigned a seat, socially distanced, for the service. The elderly, however, are encouraged to stay home. At least for the present. Sunday morning, I ready myself as I used to for the short drive to my parish. This means getting my computer set up to deliver the live feed, and it includes having the readings at hand in case the audio is not at its best. I find myself feeling at one with the First Century church—a small group of people, behind locked doors, in fear of the Romans banging on the doors.

I think of Priscilla, whose home in Rome was a meeting place for a small Christian community to meet, pray, and break bread together. Later it was a catacomb where

Christians could be buried. When I was in Rome in 1987, once again as a perita to the American delegation of bishops at the Synod on the Laity, I would sometimes take a taxi to Priscilla's place. It was quiet, and the rumblings of early Christianity could be felt. I loved the First Century feel of antiquity and endurance. On the walls, many of them concave, were early frescoes. The Virgin and child; the journey of Mary, Joseph, and Jesus to Egypt; the Breaking of Bread.

Fourteen years after Tom and I had moved to a new condo, we were pondering how to decorate a wall that was concave. Tom suggested a mural, perhaps a garden scene, and with that idea we met with a painter who listened carefully, and then suggested why not a painting of a place you know and love, a place that brings you a sense of peace. Thus Priscilla's catacombs moved center stage. Working from a good photo of the Breaking of Bread, we decided to have the painting done on canvas, which could be attached to the wall, and which would survive us.

The mural was scheduled to be installed the morning of September 11. It was quiet in our apartment, no tv or radio, and then the phone rang. Our daughter Celia asked if we were all right, and then told us the news of the attack. The installers, who were by then in our apartment, were New Yorkers whose phone calls to home could not get through. Later that day, we sat before the mural and wondered, "What would Priscilla do?"

Last week the parish deacon visited me on Sunday afternoon, with him a communion wafer, my first in months. I wept, in gratitude for the parish ministry and for the ingenious gift Jesus designed for us to be with him in the most intimate way.

Act 4

Retirement— An Ending and a Beginning

While APAH flourished, however, Tom's health deteriorated. It became clear that the responsible next step for me, acting on the truth of the moment, was to finally retire. I could not leave him for the travel the work required, and I did not want to deprive us of precious time together. So, at the end of 1997, I began the process of retirement. An emotional moment came at the General Assembly of the National Conference of Catholic Bishops where my new milestone was announced. There was a series of small receptions, newspaper stories, awards (including the Pro Ecclesia Pontifice) and conversations with bishops who over the years had shared their own stories of vocation with its existential joys and disappointments.

I left the Conference aware of the richness of experience and purpose that I had never planned for but which was so central to my mid-adult life. What to make of this? Perhaps to simply follow the golden thread.

And the golden thread led me to Woodstock Theological Center. The center, located at Georgetown University in Washington, D.C., could be described as a theology think tank. Jesuits from a variety of experiences, academic and pastoral, worked with the title of "senior fellow." There was also a layman associated with one program in particular—Business Leadership. There was support staff (mostly women) who were secretaries, accountants, and administrative assistants. The Jesuits lived "in community" in a Georgetown house which had been gifted to them. The rest of the Center's personnel lived in homes throughout the various jurisdictions of Maryland, Virginia, and the District of Columbia.

This small community of men and women worked in the realm of big ideas. It was this that attracted me to Woodstock. I had received offers from several academic institutions and dioceses to join them, but they all required moving away from the stability of place where family, friends, and familiar spaces wove a tapestry of peace and security.

Two years before my retirement from the Bishops' Conference, the Jesuits of the world had met in a "general congregation" which occurs every ten years. The gathering occurs in Rome where delegates engage in "discernment," i.e. figuring out Jesuit priorities for the following decade under the guidance of the Holy Spirit. Among the priorities of 1995 was encouraging collaboration with women in the various Jesuit missions.

My retirement and the Jesuit priorities came together.

I had several in-depth conversations with Woodstock's director, Father Jim Connor, who was hoping to inaugurate a program in Church Leadership. He believed my background with both hierarchical and lay leadership would fill the need. And I would also demonstrate that the Jesuits were serious about opening their missions to women.

It was agreed that I would come to Woodstock in the spring of 1998 as a senior fellow—the first woman resident. For the first few months of 1998 I would be "in recovery" from Conference responsibilities, and the recovery would be aided with a gift of being "writer in residence" at the Washington National Cathedral. That turned out to be the perfect bridge to a different life style. I went to what was then called the College of Preachers, located next to the cathedral, three days a week. I was given two rooms—one for work and one for rest. There was a large and interesting library, and if a retreat or study group would occur during my time there, I was welcome to join in. Once a week, Tom would come around noon, and we went out to lunch. The other days, old-fashioned peanut butter sandwiches filled the need.

It was there that I wrote a small book called *Seven Essentials for the Spiritual Journey.* The spring before I retired from the Bishops' Conference, I had delivered a Baccalaureate Address at Lafayette College in Pennsylvania. I had given many other commencement addresses, but they had all been at Catholic colleges. Lafayette was not Catholic. I researched the religious belief systems of the people who would be there at the morning service—a mixture of Christian, Muslim, and Jewish. What did they have in common besides being in the tradition of Abraham? I discovered that the common element in their spirituality was the importance of "pilgrimage." So I framed my presentation as the Essentials of the Spiritual Journey. An editor with the Crossroad Publishing Company happened upon a summary of my text in a newsletter and asked me to write a book based on it. So that's what I did at the College of Preachers. *Seven Essentials for the Spiritual Journey* was published in 1999 and has been in print ever since, aided by Boston College's on-line program based on the book.

One of the first things I noticed about Woodstock was the focus on conversation. At the Bishops' Conference, the main emphasis was the Church. At Woodstock, the conversation was about God. One of my colleagues there described it as trying to figure out what God was up to, how could we know and how could we help? It was enormously exciting—so much so that my original intention to be at Woodstock for three years kept extending. I ended up staying there 14 years. The integrity in the pursuit of those questions was life-giving.

In addition to pursuing our individual projects, Woodstock's Senior Fellows met weekly for a seminar using books recommended by one of the Fellows. But the theological method of Bernard Lonergan SJ was frequently, if not always, a backdrop. Sometimes we used a colleague's not-yet-finished manuscript, and sometimes we used a book not normally studied in theological circles. I think of Jane Jacobs, an architectural journalist best known for *The Death and Life of American Cities*. We may have been the only theological study group in the country poring over Jacobs' work on the environment. I remember those seminars as bridging our Catholic past with the ecumenical present, giving us and our work a sense of relevance.

A Fond Farewell from Archbishop Dennis Schnurr

Chatting with Archbishop Daniel Pilarczyk

Congratulations from Sister Sharon Euart, RSM

Receiving Award from Bishop Anthony Pilla

Grieving With Grace

When the worst thing I could imagine happened—namely, Tom's death—my Woodstock work with its insertion into the ongoing intellectual search and the spiritual support of my colleagues enabled me to weave hope into the web of my existence. I had a place to go to every day if I wanted to— and I did. That structure held me upright. I would enter my apartment at the end of the day having traveled home by cab (Tom used to pick me up after I lost my parking space to Georgetown Hospital). What awaited me was silence— not the silence of deep peace but the silence of emptiness. I turned to ritual for life. Light a candle. Say the Vespers of the day. Write in my journal. Write whatever came pouring forth. I determined to write something every day so I could see my life with its changes, its fears, its bits of love finding a way in. I was coming to understand that every life is flowing over with energy and history, and I was appreciating anew that it is very much about small things.

The usual grief books which help so many did not make their way into my soul, for whatever reasons. But a book by P. D. James, the English mystery writer, did. *Time to Be in Earnest* was a memoir of sorts, about her 77th year. What I found was the daily entries of a woman in her later life—a wife and mother living alone due to her husband's mental illness. It was simply an account of ordinary days and nights. P.D. James led me into the world of daily recording, and it was salvific. Because I usually wrote after praying Vespers, I began to see my experience in the light of the liturgical seasons.

Advent presented a challenge. There was the issue of the advent wreath, which has a communal feel to it. When we were a family of six—mother, father, children—everything fell into place. But now? I used a prayer I had learned when I was thirteen that ended in "grant my desires." After decades of saying that prayer, I found myself stymied. What was my desire? I recognized the importance of honesty, hearing echoes of Jesus saying to those who sought his help, "What do you want?" The older I get the more I recognize the difficulty and the importance of the question. Desire is the engine of change. And in the shadows of one's life is the question—are you ready for change? In my case, there was no choice. Tom had died. How could I live?

In the depths of my soul, I knew that the prayer of the Church, the large and growing church with its rituals and ministries, offered a pathway. With those as a structure for clarity and courage, I was drawn into this new experience of love and loss, and I was strengthened to write about it. My spiritual director, Abbot Aidan, knew I was so engaged, and he suggested that I think of the writing in terms of a book. At first, I recoiled, protective of my privacy. But then I thought about all the books and writings that had fed my soul and intellect over the years. The writers did not hoard their discoveries, but rather shared them with wider communities, something like the Gospel story of loaves and fishes. Little bits of bread and fish fed the many, and they took what they needed. And so, my struggles with life without Tom were shared in a book, *Grieving with Grace*. I remain grateful that people from many cultures and far-away places find something there to spark hope.

Surprises abounded. An English woman who lived most of the time in South Africa—the wife of an Anglican priest—appeared in my Woodstock office one day. She had read *Grieving with Grace* while coping with the death of a neighbor in her English village where she spent some of her time. The neighbor was an elderly gentleman known throughout the British Isles for his sailing prowess. For most of his adult lift—even as he aged—he was on the water, and he wrote of his experiences. By an act of God, perhaps, his writings were in the archives at Georgetown University. This woman planned to visit the Washington area to pore over these archives, and to visit me. And so, she did. More recently, I was a participant in a film retreat where we watched films unified by a common subject (i.e. "strong women") and then analyzed them in small groups. There I met a woman who had my early experience of reading the usual grief and coping books, and finally settled on my writing of personal experience. In that, she found freedom

Once again, I saw the wisdom of Abbot Aidan alive in people.

Always Smiling For Each Other

A Renewal

In the summer of 2006, I had the first conversation with Joe in half a century. I had met him back in college, when we were on a blind date arranged by a friend from TMLA. He was a track star, attending Manhattan College, a year older than I. My father adored him, and I think this figured into the "falling in love" equation. Joe was also in a Marine Corps program that required him to spend summers at Parris Island. His life pretty much revolved around athletics, but on one occasion I convinced him to accompany me to the 92nd Street Y, a venue where authors, often poets, connected with varied audiences. After all, I had attended lots of track meets. The night he came with me, Robert Frost was the featured writer. He read a great deal of his poetry which caused Joe to pivot some into the world of the arts. Later he would tell me that it was arts and athletics that sustained him throughout his life.

They say that major life changes, such as the death of a spouse or other beloved person, often lead to a review of life. It did for me, as after Tom's death, I began to wonder about the life path of my "first love," Joe, the athlete and art lover. I knew he had married, because his mother wrote to me about it. Through the years, her letters at Christmas kept me informed about his life. He had children and was engaged in his life's desired work: teaching and coaching. I never contacted him, even though Tom would say from time to time, "Send him a greeting." When Tom and I were preparing for marriage, the Jesuit who presided at our wedding counseled me never to mention Joe's name to Tom. I didn't hold to that advice, however, especially when Tom would come across an article highlighting Joe's athletic prowess, stuffed in an old envelope. Tom, always the historian, valued truthful information.

And I didn't hold to that premarital advice either, when after Tom's death, I began to wonder what life had dealt Joe. I went to the Manhattan College Hall of Fame website, and one of his sons returned my inquiry, and so plans for a reunion began.

In our first conversation, we talked first about children—Joe had four living and a son who had died of leukemia at age 12. I described my four children, two daughters and two sons. We talked about our parents, he with vivid memories of my father whom he described as "unique." That was a very consoling moment—to talk with someone who had known my father. Knowing that Tom had never met my parents was a small hole in my heart.

We talked about long-ago friends we had shared and life in New York City in mid-century. I told him about Tom and his death and the subsequent huge gap in my life. He spoke of his divorce, but with respect for his former wife then living in New England. The conversation ended with both of us saying we should arrange for a personal visit in the not-too-distant future.

I felt that a door, long closed tight, was now starting to open. I didn't think an encounter was imminent, but three days later Joe called to see if I would like company the next weekend. He would drive rather than fly or take a train because he wanted to carry with him memorabilia of a half century. There were items reflecting his work as a track and field coach—I learned that he was considered the father of track and field for Duchess County, New York. There were samples of his photography, and—most surprising—samples of his poetry. Poetry, it turned out, had sustained him over much of his adult life, something he attributed to that evening at the Y with Robert Frost so long ago.

We spent that first weekend together revisiting the connecting paths of our lives. Our shared history made it easy, and we learned bits and pieces of the lives we had enjoyed with our different families, work, vocations, and communities. He had been divorced for twenty years and retired from teaching almost as long. I, on the other hand, had been widowed for three, was still in the work force, and was still in some stage of mourning for Tom. That first "renewal" weekend we went to the Phillips Gallery in D.C., a treasure trove of modern art. We also went to Mass together, which happened to be in Spanish. He was totally confused!

He very much wanted me to see his home on the Hudson River, so I decided to drive back to New York with him. On the way, we stopped at the cemetery where much of his early family is buried, aunts and uncles I had known in our youth. It was a deeply moving experience.

That was the beginning of what my pastor called "the renewal." We would visit each other at our respective homes, meet each other's children and friends, but basically continue to live in our own residences. It was a lifestyle that appealed to me, and I assumed to Joe as well, though he would occasionally raise the subject of marriage.

And then some worrisome health issues appeared in his life that I suspected might be the beginnings of dementia. I had a conversation with a close friend of his who said Joe was exhibiting signs of Alzheimer's Disease and that he would need someone to manage his case. Joe's children were scattered around the world, and his ex-wife had her own health problems. I talked to my lawyer who had prepared our pre-marital agreement, and he directed me to an elder lawyer who offered his opinion. I could be appointed guardian, but going to court could be difficult for everyone. A better solution was to marry.

So on Memorial Day weekend, I said to Joe that I thought marriage would be good for us, but first I asked him to see a neurologist. He did, asking the doctor to call me with his findings. The substance of the phone call was that Joe did not have Alzheimer's. I took that as a sign of grace, that I should not be afraid to move on, that it was God's way of helping me overcome fear.

Joe and I married on October 8, 2008.

About a year later, the symptoms became more obvious. I was advised to take him to George Washington Hospital in D.C. where a gerontological team tested him. The results confirmed Alzheimer's. We could no longer pursue our double residence existence. Joe moved to Arlington, and I had a caregiver come three days a week while I went to my Georgetown office. Having that choice made the challenges of Alzheimer's bearable.

However, during that year, I was diagnosed with uterine

cancer, and that meant surgery and radiation. All the while, Joe's condition was worsening. When he started wandering at night, I had the locks changed. But then it occurred to me that being close in age meant that I, too, could encounter a life-threatening situation (beyond the cancer). What if I had a heart attack? Joe could no longer use a phone. My lawyer suggested residential care, and he knew of a place that was conducted in a "home" way rather than institutional. It was the model that Sandra Day O'Connor had chosen for her husband—a regular house in a regular neighborhood. Residents were limited to 6-8, and there was a staff of two to three people. The home Joe entered was spacious, with a large secure porch facing out to a garden. This is where Joe died, six months after moving in and a day after receiving the sacrament of the sick.

Once again, there was the hard work of grieving, and, in this case, arranging a funeral in New York, in Joe's beloved Hudson River Valley. He was buried in Cold Spring cemetery where so many of his family are, the cemetery we had visited a few days after our reconnection.

Within eight years, I had buried two husbands. During the early months and years after Tom's death, and during the challenge of Joe's illness and death, my work at the Woodstock Center had a salvific quality. It provided structure that was nourishing on many levels—spiritual, relational, intellectual. But as I approached my 80th birthday, with advanced arthritis and diminished energy, I knew it was time to retire—again. Time to know more deeply the life of inner space, time for a different kind of structure, time for what Abbot Aidan would call ABIDING.

Dolores and Joe's Wedding Day

Almost Done

When I began this memoir, for that is what this account really is, I was almost 86. I started it at the behest of friends who thought my life as a "first" woman in several church hierarchical entities was a story that should be told. When I finally—interiorly—agreed, I felt I had to set the scene of how a child of Irish immigrants—a girl child—made her way into unexpected places. I wanted to show how she did so in the simplest of ways. When I began, I realized that this would truly be a memoir and not an account of a woman working in the church. With every few lines, I realized that this was an attempt not only to discover and relate a true self, but to describe the worlds in which this self lived. Free-flowing writing became a form of therapy, and along the way I found myself forgiving others and understanding their lives a little better. I felt a closeness to my brother Jack, and the kindness he showed to our father and to me overtook my condemnation of his leaving his mentally ill wife.

I was old when I began this book, and now I am older. I have changed noticeably. I am in a wheelchair most of the time—a transition chair—which means I move myself around with my feet and legs. This is the result of a kitchen accident which damaged the muscles, nerves, and possibly veins on the left side of my body. The injury happened just prior to Thanksgiving 2021. It quickly pointed me in the direction of a caregiver, Cindy, who is caregiver/nurse/housekeeper five mornings a week. Her presence changes the structure of my days. No longer to I need to spend hours just trying to stay alive. There is time to pursue what I love—reading, writing, praying, thinking, meditating. There is the freedom of knowing a meal has been prepared for the evening along with a cocktail. My local children check in frequently to help me sort through financial matters and do some shopping. Sometimes we talk about our earlier lives together. We share memories of their growing up and their surviving my experimental cooking. "Do you remember Mom's tacos?" one asks. "Oh, yes," someone adds. And I add, "How about burnt green beans?" I was always afraid of undercooking.

We talk about their father and his concern about over-cooking, which led to times of undercooking—occasions for tension. We bridge our way into their current lives of work and parenting. These are life-giving conversations. They help build the house of my life.

For the last few years, I have gone to sleep reciting the Apostles Creed, recognizing it as the foundation of my life. When I come to this part—*I believe in the Holy Spirit, the holy Catholic Church, the communion of saints and the forgiveness of sins, the resurrection of the body and life everlasting*—I stop at the edge of sleep and consider the creed's last words as I have for the years since Tom died. When I wrote about that in *Grieving with Grace*, I was focused on the resurrection of the body. "In the resurrection the soul takes possession of the body as it is in God's presence in the totality the summation of its life." I found this insight of Frederick Crowe S.J. exciting, because he posits that the soul does not leave the body at all. It leaves the corpse. What Crowe does is to introduce a linguistic issue, namely the importance of translation. For the Christian scriptures, written in Greek, this is definitely important. There is a difference between a *corpse* and a *body*. I thought it so important about twenty years ago that Tom and I spent two months of summer nights studying Greek at the local community college. We went to the college four nights a week so I could read John's Gospel in the original and so Tom could revisit the Greek he learned in high school. I still think Crowe's ruminations are exciting for my late life questions. He asserts that life after death is continuous with life before, like a building erected brick by brick. He contends that after death, in the risen state, we are alive but alive with a new consciousness deriving from the vision of God. The Dominican theologian and writer Timothy Radcliff might term this "alive in God." Furthermore, Crowe's view is that nothing is ever lost. We feel loss, but what is, will always be. What we need to do, he says, is admit to our consciousness the whole reality of our span of years, including our own involvement in the universe, and to accept our selves.

This question of self-acceptance was highlighted for me in a story related by a ninety-plus woman, a protestant, who was in an ecumenical spirituality study group with the famous spiritual guide/theologian Jean LeClerc. She told him if he did not travel so much, she would ask him to be her spiritual director. He replied that if he were he would have only two points to drive home—Christ has Risen and Accept Yourself.

I wrote about all of this some years ago, and now at the edge of my own earthly life, this questioning and wisdom come back to me. I recite the Creed and understand somehow the distinction between body and corpse. Perhaps it is a question of Greek translation. Whatever, I continue to wonder about life everlasting.

Science tells us that we humans are made of matter and energy—indestructible elements. Does this mean that we all continue in some form? This seems to be part of the growing acceptance—preference even—of cremation rather than embalming and burial. Personally, I have moved from the choices of donation of my remains to a teaching hospital, to traditional burial (with a plot ready for me to be next to Tom), to cremation. The latter choice seems to fit with my growing sense that our life everlasting can be understood in terms of the planet, and perhaps beyond. Returning to earth neatly. I heard somewhere that embalming in America didn't happen until the Civil War, when so many soldiers on both sides of the conflict died away from home and from their family burial sites. The government had to find a way to return the fallen to their families. This may or may not be true, but we do know that in so many cultures the dead are buried within a short period of time or burned on the pyre or sent out on the ice to meet their end. I ponder this in these final years.

These ruminations, however, in no way invalidate my recitation of the Creed night after night. But a new question begins to form—does the resurrection of the body mean the original body? Or a changed body whose form and consciousness we have not yet figured out—if ever. I find confidence and courage in Paul's letter to the Romans.

I am convinced that neither death, nor life, nor angels, nor rulers, nor things present, nor things to come, nor powers, nor height, nor depth, nor anything else in all of creation will be able to separate us from the love of God in Christ Jesus our Lord (Romans 8:35-39).

Yes, what but in the waning years can help this awareness grow? I think music and poetry are gifts of the latter days. Not long ago I was looking around my living space and stopped at my piano—unplayed for several years. My hands now arthritic and my body in a wheel chair, I felt drawn to try to play the instrument, part of my life since childhood. My feet took the chair to the piano, and I pushed the regular bench to one side. I tried the first measure of a Mozart sonata. I could handle only two measures, and I played them over and over. That took twenty minutes. But when the time was up, there was a feeling of pure satisfaction, along with the recognition that the piano badly needed tuning. I looked up my former tuner, not knowing if he had survived Covid. He had, and he came the next week to tend to the instrument. Meanwhile, I continued to add measures, and then pages, and then a Chopin waltz. I recognized the muscle memory in my fingers, and now piano is on my daily agenda.

So is poetry, and it is more often a gateway to prayer. The long life has its own beauty. Consider this poem—

Things That Really Matter

What are they?
Who are they,
    these things that really matter?
Is it winning or losing

the tennis match,
the mayoral election,
the state lottery?
Is it success or failure
in obtaining this or that contract,
in passing the orals,
in breaking the high-jump record?
Or is what really matters
simply loving and being loved
by one's God,
by one's companions,
by one's self?

Bishop Robert Morneau

I cannot help but think of the lines in T.S. Eliot's poem, "East Coker," where he writes, "in my end is my beginning."

Sustained by Music

Further Reading

The Life of Meaning by B. Abernathy and W. Bole (Seven Stories Press, 2007)

"Is Science of Any Help in Thinking about Heaven?" by Stephen M. Barr (Church Life Journal, Notre Dame University)

The Beauty of Dusk by Frank Bruni (Simon and Schuster, 2022)

Vesper Time by Frank Cunningham (Orbis Books, 2017)

The Hours of the Universe by Ilia Delio (Orbis Books, 2021)

The Four Quartets by T.S. Eliot (Harcourt, 1943)

Grieving with Grace by Dolores Leckey (St. Anthony Press, 2008)

Interior Journey by Dolores Leckey (Twenty-Third Publications, 2015)

Is This All There Is? By Gerhard Lohfink (Liturgical Press, 2018)

Jesus Risen by Gerald O'Collins, S.J. (Paulist Press, 1987)

The Long Life by Helen Small (Oxford University Press, 2007)

The Book of Sirach in the Bible

The Book of Psalms in the Bible

Made in the USA
Middletown, DE
26 May 2023

31528782R10106